I WANT TO KNOW IF I GOT

TO GET MARRIED

SOUL WORSHIP

A Study in African-American Worship

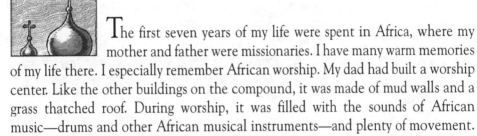 The first seven years of my life were spent in Africa, where my mother and father were missionaries. I have many warm memories of my life there. I especially remember African worship. My dad had built a worship center. Like the other buildings on the compound, it was made of mud walls and a grass thatched roof. During worship, it was filled with the sounds of African music—drums and other African musical instruments—and plenty of movement. I loved participating in African life and worship. It makes me grieve to think how Africans were snatched from their home life, their culture, and their religious rituals, to be brutally enslaved in America.

African-American worship continues to reflect the people's roots in Africa and their experience in slavery. For these reasons African-American worship has a unique place in the history of American worship. In this session we will look at African worship in the slave setting and study a clandestine worship from a slave setting. These insights will broaden our appreciation of African-American worship and bring us into contact with its rich history.

THE AMERICAN SLAVE SETTING OF AFRICAN-AMERICAN WORSHIP

African slaves were expected to worship in the same style as their owners, but they found this worship to be oppressive and depressing. For one thing, the main purpose of the sermon was usually to keep slaves under oppression, as if slavery were God's will and destiny for their lives. Slaveholders also limited the slaves' natural desire to respond to God and so limited their freedom to be open and expressive. The lack of opportunities for communal fellowship was particularly difficult for Africans because they so highly valued kinship and community in their African roots.

These restrictions forced the Africans to search out a separate time and separate space for their own kind of worship. These early attempts at separate worship were clandestine and very risky. But Africans persevered to create their own special kind of worship in the secrecy of brush arbors and "designated" cabins. This style of worship, as well as its place and time, came to be known among the slaves as "Invisible Institutions" of worship. In this way slave worship became separated from the more visible and legal places of worship that were controlled by the white slaveholders.

These services were usually conducted in late evening prayer and praise meetings that frequently lasted all night. In these secret meetings slaves felt they could meet with and respond to Jesus, who had walked a similar path of pain and sorrow.

In this setting the Africans were able to overcome their dislocation in life and be relocated in God. At work the African was addressed as "nigger," with all that the word implied. But in worship Africans entered a new society, the society of God in which they were valued as persons. Here they were no longer "niggers" but brothers and sisters. Their true home, in God, was made real in the fellowship of the church.

In the safety of this environment, Africans were able to forge their own style of worship. Here they poured out their struggles, sorrows, and pains to Jesus and to each other. Here they experienced joy in being alive and being able to meet "just one more time." Here they heard the message of liberation from Egypt. They learned how to deal with those who enslaved them, and they anticipated being released from the power of the evil one and reaching their heavenly home.

Preachers who had received the "call" of the Holy Spirit and were approved by the slave community developed a style of preaching that was full of powerful imagery and pictures, a style of sermon that was participatory and filled with story-telling narrative—one that engaged the whole person and all of the senses. As Melva Costen writes, "One does not listen simply through the ears alone; one does not see simply through the eyes only; and one's emotions can be animated by intellect, reason and intuitive sight."

The order and rhythm of worship in these clandestine meetings can be determined from slave narratives, diaries, and observers. Their worship was truly the "work of the people" enabled by the Holy Spirit in their midst. Here the community sang, prayed, preached, celebrated the Christian rituals of baptism and the Lord's Supper and enjoyed fellowship with each other.

A MODEL OF CLANDESTINE AFRICAN-AMERICAN WORSHIP

A model of clandestine African-American worship has been developed by African-American scholar Melva Costen, professor of music and liturgy at the

Prayer

Prayer seems to have been an especially important element in worship, and it also signaled a new level in the dynamics of the flow. The first of these prayers were later labeled "invocations." They expressed thanksgiving to God for allowing people to be there "clothed in their right minds." In keeping with the African tradition, there were prayers of adoration, praise, thanksgiving, intercession, and petition. Prayers after the sermon would often "drive home" the message of the sermon or exhort the congregation to live "so God could use them." It was not unusual for conversions to take place in the midst of prayers, as people continued to respond to the Word. Liberation, freedom, and deliverance were natural themes of prayers.

Preaching

The Word of God, as it was preached, heard, and experienced in a free (albeit clandestine) worshiping environment, was the foundation of the Invisible Institution. The reality of the presence of Jesus, the Word incarnate, was evident in sermon, song, and prayer. In separate environments the good news of liberation, salvation, and sanctification for *all* was quite clear. The preacher, as a divine deliverer of the Word, was responding to a call from God, combining knowledge of the Bible with the ability to communicate. Like the African *griot* (storyteller), the preacher was able to hold the attention of the people and engage them in dialogue. The role of the preacher as priest, pastor, prophet, diviner, and "chosen" leader (both by God and by the people) converged during the time for preaching. Whatever else the people expected during these clandestine gatherings, nothing was more important than the preached "word from the Lord." Although preaching styles varied, an intoned or musical delivery style was quite common. This style encouraged dialogue that would evolve into a new song.

Shouting

Shouting in worship, along with involuntary physical movements, is one way that a person responds emotionally to the movement and enabling power of the Holy Spirit. Described as religious ecstasy or "getting happy," shouting also may have involved uncontrollable screams, yells, and vocal utterances called "speaking in tongues." Shouting could occur during preaching, praying, singing or emotional personal testimonies. Although shouting was performed by individuals, the community was affected by this emotional expression; the emotions of others could become so aroused that they too would shout.

Interdenominational Center in Atlanta, Georgia. It is based on research into the narratives and diaries of African slaves. We will follow Dr. Costen's model here.

CALL TO WORSHIP

The "call to worship" started long before services began, usually announcing the time and place through the words of songs that had dual or multiple meanings. Slaves would understand that songs such as "Steal Away to Jesus," "Get You Ready, There's a Meeting Here Tonight," and "Over My Head" might have been calls to meeting or calls to escape. Either would have meant freedom from the current situation, in spite of the danger of getting caught. Certain words in the "call" might have identified the sacred space and the time for worship as well, since it was often necessary to change them.

A TIME OF GATHERING

There is evidence that slaves spent time at the beginning of worship "reconnecting" and establishing the sacred space. They would inquire about each person's state of health, what each person had been doing since the last meeting, and the whereabouts of the family. They sang, greeted, and embraced each other as they continued to worship.

SINGING

The response to God in song reflected the African propensity to engage the whole self in prayer, making it an expression of belief, attitude, and commitment. Very soft singing was apparently an extension of the call to worship, as the gathering community reconnected and became centered so that worship could take place. Words and music were shaped spontaneously or were carried over from psalms and hymns heard in Euro-American worship. The sound of slave singing has been described as wild, weird, plaintive, sorrowful, and sad.

Music and song lifted slaves closer to God and to each other as they struggled to cope with the harsh slave system. Singing at worship and at work helped to ease pain and connected the sacred with the secular dimensions of life. Singing served a symbolic, linguistic function as a common means of communicating the faith and hope of an oppressed, marginalized people. Spirituals, the first religious music created by African-Americans, communicated a spiritual depth that all people could recognize as powerful.

I WANT TO KNOW IF I GOT TO GET MARRIED

MILES FRANKEL

FLANKER PRESS LIMITED
ST. JOHN'S

Library and Archives Canada Cataloguing in Publication

Frankel, Miles, 1944-2014, author
    I want to know if I got to get married : a doctor on the Grenfell mission / Miles Frankel.

Includes index.
Issued in print and electronic formats.
ISBN 978-1-77117-393-3 (paperback).--ISBN 978-1-77117-394-0 (epub).--
ISBN 978-1-77117-395-7 (kindle).--ISBN 978-1-77117-396-4 (pdf)

    1. Frankel, Miles, 1944-2014--Travel--Newfoundland and Labrador. 2. Physicians, Foreign--Travel--Newfoundland and Labrador. 3. International Grenfell Association. 4. Missions, Medical--Newfoundland and Labrador. 5. Medical care--Newfoundland and Labrador. 6. Newfoundland and Labrador--Description and travel. 7. Newfoundland and Labrador--Social life and customs--20th century. I. Title.

R463.N44F73 2015   610.92   C2015-902003-4
                                                                 C2015-902004-2

PRINTED IN CANADA

This paper has been certified to meet the environmental and social standards of the Forest Stewardship Council® (FSC®) and comes from responsibly managed forests, and verified recycled sources.

Cover Design by Graham Blair
Edited by Robin McGrath

FLANKER PRESS LTD.
PO BOX 2522, STATION C
ST. JOHN'S, NL
CANADA

TELEPHONE: (709) 739-4477   FAX: (709) 739-4420   TOLL-FREE: 1-866-739-4420
WWW.FLANKERPRESS.COM

9 8 7 6 5 4 3 2 1

  Canada Council   Conseil des Arts
for the Arts   du Canada

We acknowledge the financial support of the Government of Canada through the Canada Book Fund (CBF) and the Government of Newfoundland and Labrador, Department of Tourism, Culture and Recreation for our publishing activities. We acknowledge the support of the Canada Council for the Arts, which last year invested $153 million to bring the arts to Canadians throughout the country. *Nous remercions le Conseil des arts du Canada de son soutien. L'an dernier, le Conseil a investi 153 millions de dollars pour mettre de l'art dans la vie des Canadiennes et des Canadiens de tout le pays.*

CONTENTS

INTRODUCTION

I was born on March 31, 1944, at Oldchurch Hospital, Romford, to the east of London. My first memory must have been a loud bang, because in the year of my birth a doodlebug bomb fell from the sky, killing the nurse attending my mother but sparing us both. Much of the rest of my life has been like that: catastrophe and rescue. The time was toward the end of World War II.

My father was German and had been arrested as an enemy alien at the beginning of the war, and summarily sent to a POW camp in Canada manned by Ukrainian guards under a brutal regimen. He survived by his kindness and medical skills.

Mother and Father were separated, but saved by my mother who for several years went from door to door collecting signatures from ratepayers and householders, and when she had 10,000 signatures her MP was obliged to act on the document. My father was released and should have stayed in Canada where a secure future awaited him, but he did not. He hitchhiked to the Maritimes and stowed away on a Liberty ship carrying grain to Liverpool, an incredibly dangerous journey. He then made his way in the dark and cold from Liverpool to London, and arrived in the middle of the night at my mother's house.

What he did then was even more unexpected. He enlisted in the British Army, becoming a lieutenant in the Royal Army Medical Corps. It immediately put him in danger as a German national in British Army uniform. If he had been captured he would have been executed. He was posted to the Middle East where he saw action as a doctor in a medical regiment, rising to the rank of Major. On furloughs back to London, first myself and then my brother Stephen were conceived.

In 1948, my father returned from the Middle East, and with his war record and general references was appointed to be a consultant in the newly formed National Health Service. He had a job for life, and made the most of the post, establishing himself as a medical force in this area. He would have preferred to become a teaching hospital consultant, but with his provenance of German and Jewish origins, he had to be content with what he had. My brother and I went to school in London at a minor public school, living at home with my mother and aunts, and life was uneventful and full of love.

My brother achieved more than I did and went to Oxford, while I was given a place at the London Hospital Medical College. I hadn't liked school, playing truant a lot and not getting the point of the specifics of any subject, but I was clever and was able to muddle through.

On the first day at medical school, I remember there were a hundred of us, boys of eighteen, and we were marched into the dissecting room, a white-tiled hall. It was brutalizing, disgusting, and Victorian. We were expected to begin immediately to dissect the dead bodies. I don't know how I passed my medical exams. Along the way I discovered the differences between the fact, the art of medicine and kindness, and I let each one inform the others.

I expected to be sent to a small hospital in a dreary part of London and that is what happened. It was Poplar Hospital in London's Docklands, and it was a great training ground. All the other Residents were from the Indian subcontinent, and there was a feeling of community, with cook-ups at night when we had full use of the kitchen.

The medical work was round the clock, with busy casualties feeding the wards. Sometimes I worked twenty hours a day for seven days at a stretch. My luck was that I could call my father if I was in difficulties, and I reckon he saved twenty or thirty lives while I was there.

After two years at Poplar I was proud of what I had achieved in turning myself into a competent doctor, but I was convinced that I had no interest in going further in the hospital service. Then one day, I saw in the *British Medical Journal* an advertisement for a travelling doctor for the International Grenfell Mission, with "interesting work in the Subarctic." I applied and got the job. Six weeks later I immigrated to Canada and transferred my medical skills across the Atlantic. It was a life-changing experience and I never regretted it.

I went to St. Anthony first, which acted as the headquarters of the mission, and was given a room. But I was the travelling doctor and hardly ever spent a night in that room. My job involved going from nursing station to nursing station and small cottage hospitals strung out along the coast. This is my account of the two and a half years I was there.

In addition to the medical work I had come to do, important parts of my personal life unfolded. I was engaged to Frances Astor, who accompanied me to Canada for a period. In fact, we married there in 1970 once I had obtained permission from the Bishop of Labrador after securing all the necessary paperwork. The Reverend Tom Moulton, who was the Rector of St. Anthony, had not thought it necessary to turn on the central heating system for such a short ceremony and the church was freezing. We had two witnesses, Meg and Reg Prentice. When it came time to get the ring onto Frances's finger, she refused to take her glove off and instead held it tightly in her fist as we made our vows.

When I returned to Europe after my time with the Grenfell Mission, I needed to find work, which came easily when Frances said that she wanted to live in Paris, as there was a job available at the American hospital there. By that time we had a sailing boat, which we named *Conche*, and we sailed up the

Seine Estuary, unstepping the mast at Rouen, and then up the river to Paris. We tied up at the Touring Club de Paris, mooring at the Pont Alexandre Trois. We spent a very happy winter, me going off on a little moped to the hospital and Frances working with an international organization. We made full use of the city, going to galleries, meeting new people, and eating and drinking well.

We then went to Papua New Guinea to help my brother who was working there as a doctor, but who wanted to do a full-time Ph.D., and needed a locum to cover his clinical obligations.

After this we bought a house and farm in Ireland, but then the idea of sailing our boat back to Canada as a pleasure trip to visit old friends in Newfoundland and Labrador came to me, and the idea became a reality. There were preparations to make and equipment to buy. We decided to go the northern route, following the winds and currents to the Faroes and Iceland, and then to Greenland. We first encountered icebergs at Cape Farewell, and went south to avoid them.

The entry into Conche harbour was one of the red-letter days of my life. The Mission plane had been tracking our boat, and when we sailed in there was a twelve-gun salute of muzzleloading, duck-shooting guns, and then a party with locals on the landing stage that went on all night.

I met Candace Cochrane, a local historian and photographer, and organizer of the Quebec Labrador Foundation, whose energies have been instrumental in bringing about this book.

My father's risk taking and my mother's persistence were remarkable and contributed to who I was. I wanted to show how I came to be independent of a system that encourages conformity. I was blessed with lots of energy. Frances was the daughter of David Astor, proprietor and editor of the *Observer* newspaper, but I made no effort to make use of the fact that I had married into an aristocratic family, who could and did offer to help me do anything I wanted.

In 1973, I became a family doctor in rural Ireland and kept going at that for nearly forty years. I travelled less but spent my time between tending to my patients and our farm. Frances and I started a family, reared four boys, and had twenty happy years before things started to go wrong, which led us to separation and the courts.

Since 1980 I have spent much of my energy on horses. Emer, my partner and confidant, introduced me to hunting, which slowly developed into a fascination with working horses. Together we have bred Percheron horses since the 1990s and survived the occasional precarious situation that living with a stallion entails.

Much of my life had been like that: disasters and rescues. I was informed I had twelve months to live when I was just halfway through my sixty-eighth year and, through doggedness and unwillingness to conform, I made it to three score and ten, a minor obsession of mine to make the dates look neat on my headstone.

My exit from this world will *nearly* be matched by my dramatic entrance, almost dying seventy years later in abrupt circumstances, with a previously undiagnosed large brain tumour. But even that was not to be, because with the kindness and efficiency of modern medicine I have been spared its malign consequences. Who knows what the future will hold?

(Publisher's note: Sadly, since writing this, Dr. Frankel passed away, in November 2014.)

PUBLISHER'S NOTE

The publisher would like to thank Candace Cochrane of the Quebec Labrador Foundation for suggesting that Dr. Miles Frankel submit his manuscript to Flanker Press.

Dr. Frankel was very ill at that time, so he was assisted by his family, Gavin Frankel, and Conor Ramsden, who also gathered together family photos that greatly enhance this manuscript, including some taken by Dr. Frankel's wife, Frances Astor.

In addition to the Frankel and Astor photographs, the publisher also wishes to thank Candace Cochrane for contributing many of her own photographs, and those taken by Nurse Joan (Jo) Cattell, of the International Grenfell Association. Nurse Cattell was a highly respected contemporary of Dr. Frankel during his time with the Association.

Thanks to Graham Blair for his cover design, and to Peter Hanes for designing the interior pages of this book, and Margo and Jerry Cranford for their keen copy-editing.

Thanks also to editor Robin McGrath, who took a special, caring interest in this project.

Garry Cranford

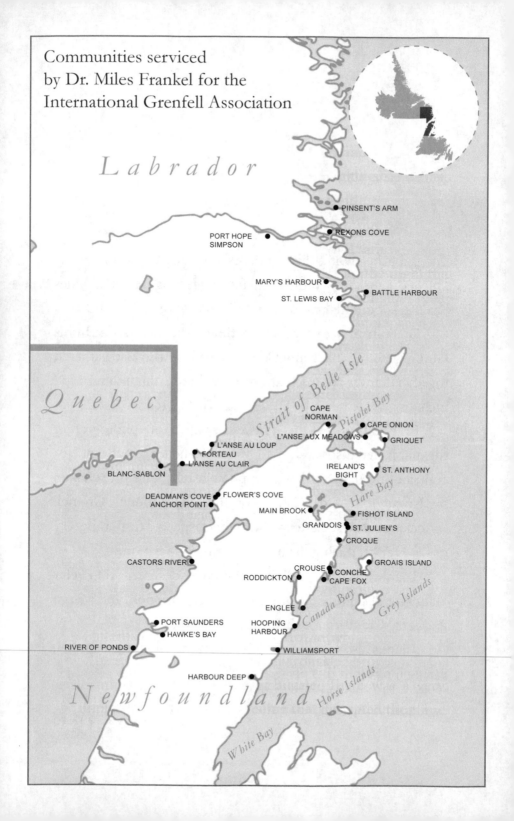

Communities serviced
by Dr. Miles Frankel for the
International Grenfell Association

Labrador

PINSENT'S ARM

REXONS COVE

PORT HOPE
SIMPSON

MARY'S HARBOUR

BATTLE HARBOUR

ST. LEWIS BAY

Strait of Belle Isle

Quebec

CAPE
NORMAN

Pistolet Bay

CAPE ONION

L'ANSE AUX MEADOWS

GRIQUET

L'ANSE AU LOUP
FORTEAU
L'ANSE AU CLAIR

IRELAND'S
BIGHT

ST. ANTHONY

BLANC-SABLON

Hare Bay

DEADMAN'S COVE   FLOWER'S COVE
ANCHOR POINT

MAIN BROOK

FISHOT ISLAND

GRANDOIS   ST. JULIEN'S

CROQUE

CASTORS RIVER

GROAIS ISLAND

CROUSE   CONCHE

RODDICKTON   CAPE FOX

Canada Bay   Grey Islands

ENGLEE

PORT SAUNDERS   HOOPING
HAWKE'S BAY   HARBOUR

RIVER OF PONDS

WILLIAMSPORT

HARBOUR DEEP

Newfoundland   Horse Islands

White Bay

THE INTERNATIONAL GRENFELL
ASSOCIATION

The organization that supported me so generously for two years was the International Grenfell Association, once a privately operated lay mission, which provided a comprehensive medical service alongside an evangelical brand of Christianity, but in recent times has been increasingly supported by the state. The headquarters of the IGA, from where the medical care and many of the social services of Northern Newfoundland and the Labrador Coast are supervised, is at the base hospital in the town of St. Anthony. On the coast, where the word "mission" did not have the paternalistic overtones that made outside journalists so angry from time to time, the IGA is still called by many the Grenfell Mission: I was the mission doctor, the wharf in St. Anthony was the mission wharf. Hymn singing and church services were broadcast daily on the hospital's Tannoy public address system and reached all administrative offices and wards except the intensive care unit and the operating theatres. No doubt at one time there was real evangelism, but by 1970 the fervour was more established and less assertive. Now that the state pays the bills, the need for parsimony and improvisation – an attraction for missionary spirits – no longer exists, and the greater staff needs of a modern medical service has brought about an intermingling of denominations and religions. Nowadays the mission hospital is staffed by Catholics, Protestants, Buddhists, Jews, Marxists, atheists, and "don't knows."

Wilfred Grenfell, an Englishman, came to the British colony of Newfoundland after having qualified as a doctor at the London Hospital in Whitechapel. His first trip, as a medical officer on a mission to the summer fisheries of the Labrador Coast, was one of those fateful meetings of the right man in the right place at the right time.

There was the man, powerful-looking and energetic, armed with lively sacraments of both evangelical Christianity and medicine. And there was the coast, a thousand miles of poorly charted bays and inlets, with secret pockets of trusting people starved of medical and spiritual guidance. The two were made for each other. The coast became one of the world's last outposts of Victorian paternalism. Grenfell had the ability to dramatize and romanticize, and the coast provided characters whose needs were starkly simple, and wild, frosty settings to thrill his comfortable Edwardian audiences. Wilfred Grenfell was an excellent fundraiser, and he put his mission on a sound financial basis through his own efforts. At the same time, both on and off the coast, he made himself into a slightly mysterious, heroic figure.

At Battle Harbour on Southern Labrador, and then at the fine natural harbour of St. Anthony, he employed local labour to build wooden hospitals, and, around these first buildings (some of which are still standing) there sprouted communities of doctors, nurses, helpers, and volunteers. On the wild, treeless, rocky coast these hospital communities were outposts of the English way of life. Lawn mowers arrived on the desolate scene, together with the medical equipment, and cows were shipped in to provide milk for the missionaries' tea, roast beef for their Sunday lunches, and the basis of a local farming industry.

Before the days of roads, aircraft, or telephones, the doctors who first worked with Dr. Grenfell were completely cut off from the outside world. The arrival of the first ship after the breakup of each winter's ice must have been a tremendous event, ending as it did five months of unbroken isolation; these days, in St. Anthony at least, it hardly creates a greater stir than the splashes of its own wake.

Throughout the winter the English way of life was maintained, bolstered with set routines and a carefully preserved parochial atmosphere, partly as a protection against a different world, partly to provide a solid base for the hard, dedicated work of setting up and maintaining an effective medical and social service.

The Newfoundlanders themselves hardly penetrated this world, which was always infused with the genteel atmosphere of an Edwardian church outing. The locals had an indifference to anything so foreign to them, and they felt unwelcome in the drawing-room atmosphere of the mission. It was inevitable that they should compare themselves with the missionaries and that the comparison should be generally, if superficially, unfavourable; by contrast, Newfoundlanders led primitive lives and were for the most part illiterate. If they were received by the mission, they felt awkward in returning the invitation to houses that were small and without sanitation or other refinements of modern times. This situation, based as it was on misunderstanding on both sides, had led to much bitterness. It explains why many people of the coast remain wary of the mission personnel, in spite of the fact the Newfoundlanders are no longer poor or without education. Many patients that I met seemed to feel that they had little in common with their doctor other than a mutual interest in their disease.

And yet, away from St. Anthony and the base hospital, the relationship between the coast and the mission had been a good one, for the doctors have always had to travel and live in the outports. In order to survive and be comfortable, the doctors and nurses had to learn the ways and customs of life on the coast; in order to do their work well, they had to become familiar with the strange uses of language; in order to travel they had to live on small boats and to learn to drive a team of dogs, in close contact with their guides. Natural human sympathies were given a chance to erode the barriers of the hospital world.

All along the coast Wilfred Grenfell built little hospitals that were visited regularly by doctors and staffed permanently by nurses. They were called nursing stations. The nurses acted as general practitioners, held clinics, went out on house calls, and tended to their own in-patients. They had a well-stocked pharmacy and prescribed drugs as they thought fit. They did their own midwifery, from antenatal care to delivery, and referred anyone whom they thought ought to see a doctor either to the travelling doctor or to the base hospital. The nurses were practically all English, England and Australia being virtually the only English-speaking countries that trained midwives at that time.

When the atmosphere of the base hospital had become more clinical, and the pioneering spirit of the early days that thrived on adventure and medical hardship had been displaced by more esoteric excitements of modern, well-run wards, intensive care beds, and radiology and pathology departments, the original spirit of Grenfell's movement continued to live on in the nursing stations; and it was in the nursing stations that I lived and worked.

It is part of the evolutionary history of all missions, or of most foreign aid, that, if it is successful, it should eventually become redundant.

When the last person who knew Grenfell had died, when the takeover of the hospital's administration by the provincial government was complete, and nothing was left of the old times except a few vestigial traditions and an occasional reminder from Grenfell's gravestone on Fox Farm Hill, the Grenfell Mission, as I knew it at the end of its life, was dead, too. But its life was a useful one, and it affected countless people.

TWO DAYS ON A MEDICAL TRIP

There had been an accident in Port Hope Simpson, two hours away by skidoo. I had been holding a clinic with the nurse in Mary's Harbour, a winter community on the Southern Labrador. All day there had been a coming and going from the nursing station, the waiting room full with a procession of modest, almost secretive people who sat in turn in the black leather chair with the headrest for dentistry. With each there had been barriers of strangeness, different language idioms, and a natural reticence about symptoms. They coped with the difficulties in their own ways, comprising a spectrum from frank clowning to the painfully tongue-tied, but I had seen many of them a dozen times before and that made the day much easier for all of us. The atmosphere had been more domestic than clinical. There had been a great exchange of gossip, the padding about of stockinged feet, the larking of some children and the crying of others, the bantering from the "aide" who mopped up melting snow from the linoleum. She was a local girl and probably related to half of them.

"What's the matter with you, Uncle Jonas? Ain't your woman giving you enough to eat? You look wonderful poor to me. Doctor's gonna take you away in his airplane and feed you up in the hospital."

"Enough of your brazen talk, maid," said Uncle Jonas. "I'm a hard case of the sugar diabetes, and the doctor's keeping me thin for a purpose. I eats according to a diet, or there'll be no way to cure me up except by needles, and that's handy on the last thing I wants."

It was four-thirty and almost dark outside, and still the skidoos were coming, their headlights pitching and flashing on the spruce trees outside the clinic window. I stopped for a cup of coffee and drank it in the waiting room, talking to a man who had brought along his mother for me to see.

Then there was loud talking outside and three men clattered up the steps into the nursing station, scarves around their faces, ice and dusty snow over their eyebrows and the fur of their hats. Their entrance was sudden and dramatic, and they were half aware of this, although they spoiled the effect by attempting, in automatic deference, to brush a little snow from their boots. One of them took off his hat, smiled a shy greeting to the nurse, and then turned to me.

"You the doctor?"

Another of them said, "Feller got his arm cut off in Port Hope Simpson. We wants fer you to come and take a look at he."

"Is the arm right off? What did he do it with, a chainsaw?"

"Some of the boys took him down to Mrs. Penny's and we came right on. I ain't a doctor, but it looks bad to me. Mrs. Penny put clean linen on and the blood soaked all on through."

I stood in the waiting room thinking of what I would need to take, of clothes to wear, of the forty miles through the forest trails, of the wounded man and his frightened attendants. The cozy, homely atmosphere of the nursing station was shattered, and the realities of the coast were to hand: isolation and suffering.

The nurse had already begun to collect together instruments and drugs and to put them into a big komatik box. We took the notes of other patients whom we could see while we were in Port Hope Simpson and all the paraphernalia for a normal clinic. Into the box went many of the bits and pieces that were to be found in modern casualty and outpatients departments: electrocardiogram apparatus, a bottle of dried plasma, and packs of sterile surgical instruments. We were chancing the frosty evening in taking a bottle of fluid for intravenous infusion because, like all drugs in vials for injection, it was likely to freeze and shatter. The temperature outside was seventeen below zero, Fahrenheit, forty-nine degrees of frost. We contacted St. Anthony on the radio telephone and asked for a plane on the following day, with a medical student or nurse to escort the patient back to the hospital. A message was sent out across the harbour for two guides who would bring us back when the affair in Hope Simpson was over, and they arrived at the nursing station, ready to go before I was even dressed.

The waiting room was still full, although everyone knew that the clinic was over, and any disappointment at not being seen was taken with good humour, as part of their involvement in this drama. They all knew the injured man, his wife and family. They all knew the appalling effects of the loss of a limb in a community that could only maintain itself through hard physical work.

Then we were all dressed to go, and, sweating under all my layers, I hurriedly ate a piece of cake while the boxes were lashed onto the komatiks, behind the skidoos of our guides. I sat astride one of these boxes and worked my gloved hand under the rope for a handhold. The nurse took the station skidoo. The six machines were started, one with difficulty involving consultation about oil in the carburetor, and the lights grazed the trail marks ahead. Then we were off over the harbour ice in a confusion of flurried snow and bitter wind: a sudden, unaccustomed movement forward into nothing. There was the exhilaration of being out of control as I bumped and swerved along behind my driver. The other five skidoos were jumbled in various formations, and the night and the flying snow in my eyes made any coherent impression impossible. With my head on one side I blinked away the snow and received flash shots of muffled men, heads down and squat as we travelled on the ponds, and others kneeling, leaning to balance their machines on the necks of land. I began to get cold as the sweat caused by the rush of preparation froze on my face and neck.

There was the apprehension of what I would find in Port Hope Simpson, at worst a man in shock with a traumatically amputated arm. As the cold night whisked by, armed with specks of ice that stung my face, I tested myself on the anatomy of the arm, muscles, blood supply, and nerves. I wished I had done more accident surgery. I planned the way we would use our equipment under the conditions we would find and, like someone off on holiday, had intermittent panic attacks that we had forgotten something. Except that instead of cufflinks and toothpaste I was worrying about morphine and a sphygmomanometer.

We got into formation on St. Lewis Bay, twenty miles of unobstructed, frozen sea, following the fresh tracks made earlier as they came into the jerking arena of our headlights. My driver turned his head every now and again to make sure he had not lost the doctor, and the nurse on her skidoo drove up alongside to yell some encouragement. Her words were snatched away into the night. We must have been going thirty miles an hour, but the sensation of speed had nothing to do with prosaic figures.

Then we left the bay and moved onto Bartlett's Trail, a steep climb, and I walked to warm myself, stumbling in the packed snow, leaning on the komatik and holding on. The trail was a peep-show tunnel of bowed spruce trees submerged in snow, and after an hour we reached the end of it and saw the welcoming sprinkle of lights at Port Hope Simpson below us.

As we entered the settlement, dogs barked, rows of children's heads appeared at dimly lit windows, and we collected an escort of boys on more skidoos. There were serious-looking men and women around the door of the Pennys' house, and more inside, in the kitchen. The patient lay on the daybed, pale, with eyes half open and a swath of bloodstained, torn linen bandage over his right side. Now the action was up to me.

The kitchen was full of friends and relations of the injured man, and the schoolmaster and Pentecostal minister were there to represent advice and knowledge. Their eyes gave unconcealed thanks that a more specific education had arrived. I was nervous of what existed under the bloody covering, and took stock of the man's general condition while the nurse exercised Labrador diplomacy to get rid of everyone but the man's wife, the Pennys, and a girl who had done a correspondence course in practical nursing.

"That was careless of you, Ambrose."

"Sir?"

"You should go easy with the chainsaw. You've got a lot more wood to cut this winter."

In spite of his pain he smiled. His lips were very pale. I lifted the coverings on the arm and found that the muscles were cut to the bone on the forearm in two places, and that there was another deep laceration over the mid-biceps. The muscles of the upper arm were flayed and there were bone chips in both wounds. There was no sign of any further bleeding. His pulse was barely perceptible and a blood pressure taken on the other arm was low.

"It's a hard pain, sir, something shockin.'"

I gave him a quarter of a grain of morphine by intramuscular injection that the nurse had already prepared by dissolving a pellet in water. We set up a drip with our plasma, which had survived the trip. The right hand looked bloodless and there was no radial pulse or sensation on that side. The edges of the lacerations were ragged and without skin along much of their length, which is always the way with chainsaw injuries. He was probably going to lose that arm from below the elbow.

After the morphine he slept uneasily while we cleaned his wounds, sutured the upper one, made a splint with a backslab of plaster of Paris, and loosely bandaged the whole arm with sterile dressings. We started a course of soluble penicillin.

We cleared the table of our rubbish and put our instruments to boil on the stove. Mrs. Penny laid the same table for supper, and we sat down to eat spruce partridge with potato and turnip.

"Lord, bless this food and us," said Mr. Penny, "and we give thanks that You sent the doctor and nurse here to help Ambrose. For Christ's sake, Amen."

We ate keeping an eye on the patient who appeared to be sleeping peacefully. His wife sat beside him as if she was in mourning, huddled and expressionless, rocking slightly. Toward the end of the supper a steady stream of visitors came into the kitchen. They entered without knocking, and with a nod of greeting sat themselves on a row of chairs against a wall, or stood by the door, their solemn attention shared equally between us at the table and the sleeping Ambrose on the daybed. They asked if we were going to hold a clinic that night or if we would visit someone ill at home.

By this time it was almost ten o'clock, and we said no to a clinic, but we were told of an old man on the other side of the settlement who had been ill for some days, and I went out to visit him. His daughter who lived with him had come to fetch me, and together we walked over the beaten snow between the houses.

"He's awful choked up on his stomach, Doctor, and don't seem to have no mind for nothing. I done what I can for him, but it be pitiful to see him like that, I calls it."

Her voice was strong and raucous, contrasting with the rest of her, which was thin and tired-looking. She was dark-complexioned with straight black hair held back with an elastic band, and there were signs of Indian or Inuit blood in the broad set of her cheeks and slanting eyes.

"He don't do his water none too good," she said quickly as we neared the house, "but he won't talk much about that."

The house was a poor one, of unpainted spruce with a tarpapered roof over one storey. The latch on the inside of the plywood door was lifted by a length of cord through a hole in the door. Inside it was very warm, almost stifling from the heat of the wood stove which crackled and spit and glowed dull red. There was an area worn through to the floorboards in the linoleum in front of the stove. A modern table with a plastic top and plastic, tubular legs and a roughly made wooden cot were the only movable pieces of furniture. A naked baby lay sweating in the cot near the stove, and the patient sat fully clothed on the daybed, leaning forward and taking his weight on his hands, labouring for breath. The room was lit, and further heated, by a hissing paraffin lamp, and in its spitting yellow shadow it was difficult to be sure of the man's colour, but his hands and lips appeared blue. He didn't look up when I came in.

"Doctor's come t'see yer, Dad," said the girl, quickly tidying the table and then taking the baby into her arms, rocking it automatically. Even in the sauna atmosphere of this kitchen the man was wearing a thick woollen shirt and two felt-like vests, and undressing him was exhausting for both of us. He had caught the flu that was going round about a month back and couldn't get clear of it. Now he couldn't even walk across the room. A nurse, or maybe a doctor, had given him some heart pills a few years back, but when the packet was finished he hadn't bothered to renew them.

When I examined him, all signs of gross congestive heart

failure were present but he would not consider going into hospital. We could have put him on the plane with Ambrose. I didn't push the idea of hospital very forcefully, because it lacked realism and, under the conditions of this man's suffering, seemed to belong to a world apart. It was a strenuous step for a person to take, to leave Port Hope Simpson for the unknown in St. Anthony, with all its associations of terminal illnesses and telegrams in the night. And so I glanced easily away from the proposal, concentrating on the treatment we would give him at home. I pressed into the puffy swelling of his ankles and told him his body was waterlogged and that his heart was under strain. I was sitting beside him with my hand resting on the thick grey felt of his trousers, squeezing his leg as I talked. One sensed that the bridges of contact were few and shaky, and that all the approaches of suggestion and persuasion might need to be brought into play. If modern medicine was out of his experience, how could he rally his will to recover at its altar? How could he pin his hope on digoxin and diuretics when they came as neatly pressed pills, sacraments of a religion that wasn't his own? I told him that treatment would give strength to his heart and kidneys and make the "dropsy of his foot wrists (ankles) pitch back." He must pass his urine often or it would stop altogether and damage his kidneys. If he didn't do what he was told, I said, he would probably die within the next week.

He understood my directness, my touch on his leg, and my sincerity, even if he couldn't make out much of what I was saying. The girl put her baby down and plugged a bottle into its mouth while she walked back to the Pennys' house with me. How old was she? Twenty-five, thirty, or thirty-five? She had a quick, shy smile that lit up her face. Several of her front teeth were missing and many of the others were rotten. When she smiled, her expression was ribbed by the lines of drudgery and the general abuse of a hard life. She was unmarried and nursing her father under difficult conditions. The house needed water and fire, heavy pails lifted from the stream through the deep ice, wood carried from the pile and chopped into splits for the stove. Her baby needed clean nappies and warmed bottles of milk. She was shivering as we went into the Pennys' kitchen.

"How's the baby, Dorcas?" asked the nurse.

"She's some smart now, Nurse." She nodded as we gave her instructions for her father's care, and she took the treatment back with her across the snow path to the little house at the edge of the settlement. Ambrose was still sleeping and the drip was going in well. He had no fever. His wife had left to look after their seven children.

Then I stood out in the frosty night, talking to Mr. Penny. The sky was filled with the majestic, shifting drapery of the Northern Lights. That night's were the best I had ever seen. Our talk was hushed, almost awed whispers, and our boots crunched in the snow that stretched out from the Pennys' front door into the bay. The long straight bay had become the nave of a cathedral, its roof vaulted with the ghostly symmetry of the phosphorescence of the Aurora Borealis. As we took all this in, the night crystallized our breath and was very still, except for a gargoyle moon which rose from the hill to the left of the bay to complete the picture. It was very likely that the weather would hold and that the airplane would make it to us in the morning, a thought that brought me no little pleasure.

"You going to have a lunch before you go to your bed, Doctor?" I had one more long look at the Northern Lights, which had now shifted and were wavering at the end of the bay like searchlights, and went back into the kitchen, glad for the warmth.

"For these Your gifts we give You thanks, Lord Jesus," said the nurse, and we ate fruitcake and drank a cup of tea. Ambrose was now more a part of the company, although as the morphine wore off he was having more pain. His eldest son, a boy of about fourteen, who had been working with his father on a new trap boat for next summer's fishing, had come to sit with him. He had fair hair, cut short, and wore clean, pressed jeans and an open-necked shirt, and he listened intently as we talked. At his age he would be expected to do a man's work, and the expression on his oval, Nordic, boy's face was of one who was accustomed to responsibility.

We gave Ambrose a further sixth of a grain of morphine while Mrs. Penny washed up with water from the stove. Then I went upstairs to bed in the Pennys' house, which had become our hospital. The nurse sat with Ambrose and his son in the warm kitchen, dozing from time to time, checking the progress of the intravenous infusion, giving him his injection of penicillin. We all woke up with his screams as she sat him up to help him pass his urine, and in only my long underwear I groped down the stairs to see what was going on. It was dawn and I was dismayed to find a low cloud ceiling over the bay. Ambrose had a temperature of a hundred degrees Fahrenheit, but he looked well and his pulse and blood pressure had remained steady.

"When did the weather come down?"

"This old arm will come off in St. Anthony, not Hope Simpson," said Ambrose, to cheer me up. "It'll be good on the outside, and the mission plane will find us under that cloud."

He was right. His wife arrived with a bag for him to take to the hospital, and the kitchen filled with men who carried him over the ice to the plane. Then at the far end of the bay we saw the unmistakable shape of the de Havilland Beaver aircraft and watched it land along the line of small spruce trees frozen into the harbour ice. A stretcher was brought from the aircraft and we loaded our patient onto it. The pilot was a friend and we talked to him and shared a bar of chocolate, our shadows reaching almost to the settlement in the early morning sun, which had burnt off the thin cloud.

With Ambrose delivered to an expert surgeon working in conditions more suited to his art than Mrs. Penny's kitchen, we were left to enjoy our morning. We held a clinic and saw people known to us, who let us know they were still on treatment and felt mostly well. We heard news and were given other news to pass on. I again visited the man in heart failure and found him no worse and in much better spirits. The drive back to Mary's Harbour with our guides was in the warm winter sun. The wide freedom of the forest and the frozen sea were no longer a threat.

WINTER, AND A MAY TRIP TO
CASTORS RIVER

Labrador has two seasons, I was told: winter and July. Apologetic humour accounted for much of my welcome to Newfoundland. My new friends had watched generations of Englishmen shiver in the north wind and knew that England's climate must be milder. But as I shivered, I also sweltered; there is a summer and it can be hot. The winter and the summer are as different as the two faces of the moon.

The change in temperature gives the country two separate identities, the one at first sight having little to do with the other. It is difficult to reconcile the joy of sailing down the coast on a balmy summer's day with one's memory of the same place in winter; then we were struggling with a team of dogs over the sea ice, catching glimpses of the black rocks through a blizzard. But the ice age recedes every year, and the summer flowers blossom without recrimination. For all its harshness and violence, the winter disappears without a trace.

Northern Newfoundland and the coast of Southern Labrador have technically a climate described as Subarctic – icy winters, but not insupportably cold, and summers long enough for the snow to melt. The area shares the same latitude as Southern England, but whereas the English climate is modified by the warm, moist tropical Gulf Stream, Newfoundland has to contend with the Labrador Current: a stream, never very wide, that flows from the deep-freeze of Baffin Bay, southward along the Labrador Coast to the Davis Straits and the Labrador Sea, and on to Newfoundland, which it embraces in two cold arms, one stretching through the Strait of Belle Isle and the other around to the east coast. It is this icy hug that makes the Englishman shiver. But when a ridge of high pressure settles over the country, a temporary block against the familiar depressions, and the Gulf Stream lazily flicks its tail northward, the effect of the Labrador Current is neutralized; the land can become hot like the desert. When I climbed on to the merry-go-round of the seasons it was the beginning of winter, or freeze-up as it is called.

Most of the people I knew considered themselves fishermen, or the wives and children of fishermen. It is true that most of their livelihood came from the sea; they lived on the coast and their customs, expressions, and history were those of seafaring people. But winter lasts six months, freezing the inshore waters, and for more than half the year they were unable to fish. On the shore that I knew, winter was a tremendous disruption to people, meaning six months compulsory shore leave every year with nothing to offset a monotonous existence and diet other than personal initiative and energy. To the degree that these qualities were lacking in any individual, he or she suffered accordingly. The women, more confined than the men, kept most of the time in the houses with little or no change of company in the outports, were the most affected. As the winter drew on I noticed that I prescribed more calmants and tranquillizers than I did at other times of the year, and my "sample of one" is borne out by official figures published by the provincial government.

But for those who could cope with redundancy, whose reaction to the alternatives is energetic, the winter was welcoming. And these people, as a result of natural selection, were in the majority. The need to survive encouraged positive thinking, and the fact that many generations had survived implied that this quality was being passed on. The summer presented you with work: in the winter you had to go out to look for it.

Medicine is only seasonal in a limited sense, and the clinics were much the same, even if the snow was twenty feet deep outside the window, which made me less affected by winter than most. But even so . . .

St. Anthony

Full up with moose steaks. I have just come down on the *Bar Haven* (the coastal steamer) from the clinic at

Harbour Deep. I had to wait until midnight before I knew the steamer was coming, and when we saw her lights turning round the head of the bay, Nat (the nursing station foreman) came to collect me. Because the ice conditions down the shore (meaning the north) were not known, the skipper decided not to leave until dawn. Chesley Pittman, who owns the wharf and the store, and who controls much of Harbour Deep's domestic and foreign policies, came down to see the *Bar Haven*'s skipper, with a couple of rabbits and an otter skin as gifts. I had a glass of rum with them before I turned in.

In the dawn the sea had an oily, monochrome look to it, like a photograph out of focus. The great Atlantic rollers were pressed flat by a colloidal surface suspension of early ice. As we rounded the point and headed north I saw the waves heaving over the rocks like molasses, without breaking. The ship pushed against the water rather than cleaved it, and the bow wave was pushed up like a padded halter. The propellers churned the dense water, which made me think of grey whipped cream. This is what is called slob ice, and somehow it's a good name. The skipper told me that old-timers used, in necessity, to propel their boats through it with a plank nailed at right angles to the end of a long, stout stick of wood, a piece of equipment called a slob hauler, pulling their craft up the pole toward the plank which found a purchase in the gelatinous water.

Sails and small outboard motors were no good in slob, which, unlike later ice, will not support weight, and to be stuck in slob ice can be more of an annoyance.

As we went north the slob became denser, as if frog spawn was covering the bleak Atlantic as far as we could see. It formed little blobs of ice the size of marbles, and then, more to the north, these seemed to join to form diminutive pans of ice, looking just like the leaves of water lilies, the same size and with upturned edges.

We put into Englee to deliver the last freight of the year. Behind Englee Island there was firm ice about eighteen inches thick, covered with a thin layer of snow. The ship ground a channel through it, quickening the ice with snaking fissures, and came to rest a half-mile offshore, our channel filled with bobbing slabs of frozen, crazy paving. We loaded the freight, mostly building materials, onto the ice, and anyone expecting something walked out from Englee on snowshoes, or drove a skidoo. Until then I had been the only passenger, because people don't move around much at freeze-up – the return trip is always doubtful – but at Englee a few joined the ship.

We backed out of the ice, slamming and rebounding against the banks of the channel we had made coming in, and continued north to Conche, Croque, and St. Anthony. At Conche, with the slob thickening and with the possibility of having to turn back – or even to be stranded throughout the winter – the captain very kindly agreed to wait half an hour while I saw a patient that the nurse had radioed had suffered a stroke, or something like one. It was an elderly woman and we decided to let her take her chances at home. They wouldn't have wanted her in St. Anthony anyway, because she needed nothing but nursing care and her daughter would have to do that. There is a great need here for an old people's home and geriatric care, but in the absence of facilities they have to care for each other.

In St. Anthony, where we arrived at four this afternoon, the ice was so thick that the heavy ship took fifteen attempts at ramming, and reversing to ram again, to beat a channel through it to the government wharf.

Once the ice and snow has come it does not go away. It covers the land and sea with a press of all the colours of white and stays for five or six months. But if it is a disruption it is an ally as well, asphalting the country with the possibility of travel in any direction, skidoos and dog teams using the land, the ponds, and the frozen sea in the same unconfined way as boats on the water. The roads become an adventure, not to be undertaken lightly: deep canyons and tunnels through drifts of packed snow, or skating rinks like Dutch canals. The highway can become impassable within minutes, converted by a fall of snow and the wind into a series of cul-de-sacs, and an hour's journey can take a night, or have to be postponed for a couple of days.

Flower's Cove, January

It has snowed heavily in the past two days, and there were drifts against the Land Rover six feet deep. I should not have parked outside. As a result of my carelessness, I had to dig it out of its hole wearing snowshoes. I tried to use the front winch to pull it out, but the tree snapped off where I tied the rope as if the sap had frozen and made it brittle. The lock on the door was blocked by ice, and I lost some skin from my upper lip trying to melt the ice by blowing. I froze directly on the metal. The blood wouldn't clot in the cold, and the snow around the Land Rover began to get red, although I felt no pain. After a struggle I was pulled out finally by the Dept. of Potholes (Highways) bulldozer man, name of Moses, I think he said. Moses told me of the classical way to unfreeze a door lock, and when he had gone I tried out his method with success: urination from a distance of not more than two feet. I suppose that makes this a man's country after all.

I drove to Flower's Cove and went off the road twice. Four-wheel drive and tire studs don't help much when the breeze catches me on the broad reach. Once I was blown sideways when standing still at the top of the hill, just as I was wondering how on earth I was going to get down it. The grader (the huge snowplow and road surfacer) had managed to keep the road open, but it was only one track wide, and passing would be a problem. Not that it was today. Not a soul was about this morning except Sam at the strip. I had to wait for the grader at Watson's Brook because the road was blocked and I reckoned I had had enough digging for the day. The sun came up over the marshes like photographs of the moon, still and lifeless and full of sharp shadows. The grader operator was called Aaron, but was no relation to Moses. I shared a cold bottle of beer with him, full of icy spicules.

It took me four and a half hours to reach Green Island Brook, where I stopped at John Hughes's house for a lunch to give the grader operator a head start. John senior is away in the woods toward Main Brook, cutting and sawing lumber. Went off the road again at Sandy Cove and visited Grandfather White while two of his sons pulled me back on and put chains on the wheels. It cost forty dollars. I had another lunch and a glass of whisky with Grandfather White.

Heather (the nurse at Flower's Cove) was surprised to see me because she had heard the road was blocked. There was no problem to arrange a clinic because the telephone was jammed by people who had seen my jeep following the grader, and before I had finished my coffee the waiting room was full.

Roddickton, January

The clinic ended at six o'clock yesterday evening at Flower's Cove. After a dental extraction I had trouble in stopping heavy bleeding from a tooth socket and had to put a suture in. The patient – a strong youth of twenty – wouldn't keep still, nervous because he thought he was losing too much blood. In the struggle I managed to sew his tongue to his right cheek, and had to have another go. He bit my left index finger and Heather gave me a tetanus shot.

I decided to come on to Roddickton because the forecast said the weather was coming down. It did – as I was driving there.

At one point I thought I was going to be all night. Very sinister in the headlights, drifting claws of snow groped across the road and shook the vehicle as I slammed into them, and I was continually changing gear to get up enough speed to barge through the next one. Then the snow in the air and the visibly creeping drifts obliterated the road, distorting my perspective on the location of the roadway. I don't know how I kept on the road, or perhaps I didn't, and didn't know it. For a while, on the road through the country, I had to dig through a drift, but the more I sweated the faster it grew, and I decided to go back. But after turning the jeep, which involved more digging, the headlights lit up a flow of lava-like snow, suddenly blocking the road behind me. I reversed in anger into the darkness, at full speed through the trench I had already dug, and barged away through the last obstruction. I ended up plodding along in low gear ratio and didn't arrive in Roddickton until two this morning.

I saw a big white owl on the road, wings outstretched over a dead rabbit, and two bright green eyes. I had to stop because she blocked the road. All around were the skeletons of birch and spruce trees from a forest fire some years back, and the whole scene, owl and trees and flaying snow, was bizarre. I think my finger is beginning to swell from the bite yesterday.

Roddickton, January

We have been pleasantly snowed in for two days. Even the telephone is out of order. We kept the radio telephone on all day to see how everyone else is doing. There is a spirit of beleaguered friendliness as we listen to each other's weather. Mary's Harbour seems to be having an icy hurricane.

We have two cases of pneumonia in at the moment, one lobar and the other broncho, as well as two "midder" cases. One delivered in the night – while I slept! – and the other is having pains now. She should be in St. Anthony.

She had a postpartum hemorrhage with the last one, but she kept quiet about it, and now the weather has stranded her here. We'll have a fright if she hemorrhages, so I am annoyed with her in anticipation, but I must not confuse ignorance with innocence. We also admitted a child from Main Brook with deep jaundice. She is drowsy, and worries me, too.

Clinics have been busy. With the impossibility of referral I have had to be more on my mettle, and have been doing things I would have avoided if the aircraft was flying or the roads were open. I have reduced a Colles fracture (of the wrist) – never done that before without an X-ray. I cauterized the cervix of a woman whom, earlier, I certainly would have sent to the gynecologist. I exorcised a lymphoma from a man's back, an operation that grew in stature as it proceeded, involving artery forceps and the station's entire stock of sterile swabs to mop up the blood. My diagnoses had to stand on their own, their backs to a wall of first principles, without the support of investigations or the opinion of a colleague. It is tiring not being able to pass the buck. We are going to Englee tomorrow, weather permitting. My finger is definitely infected and is beginning to throb. "A man bit me, Doctor!" I am on penicillin but keep forgetting to take the pills.

Englee, January

The clinic at Englee was hell. I saw eighty-six patients, and the nurse several others in the waiting room and in the passage outside my room. We ran out of rubber gloves, sterile instruments, penicillin, and Librium. I slept well in spite of my bad finger, but woke in the night for unexplainable reasons when it stopped snowing.

During my time there, Newfoundland had the highest death rate by accident of all the provinces of Canada. It was also the largest producer of primary products. It is the country's climate, especially in the period leading into and out of winter, that connects these two statistics. Accidents at freeze-up and breakup in the lumber woods and at the fisheries were as inevitable as the stream of casualties at a hospital by a motorway, or behind the front line of a battle. And each death had a sting to it that was shared through all the interrelated communities.

Fox Harbour, January

This is the eighth day of the trip (by dog team). The weather came down on the way from the Arm (Pinsent's Arm), and now it's blowing a gale. There was a very unpleasant incident this evening that disrupted the clinic at George Poole's house, and almost left me with two death certificates to sign. We had a woman earlier in the evening, and two hours after she had left we were given word that she had not returned home. Her son had fetched her by skidoo, and although their house wasn't far away, the two of them were missing.

The storm was of incredible violence. Snow was being whirled and sluiced between the houses in such solid quantities that the porch light was invisible from three feet outside. Alone in the swirling dark, I too lost my way in seconds as the storm held up its magnets to my sense of direction. Worse still, there was a Venturi effect in the wind that sucked my breath, and in the struggle to regain it I had turned through a half circle, or perhaps more, and was even more lost. But I was found, only yards from the house, and led back to George's kitchen, and I left the searching to people who could find their way by the feel of the land, instinctively.

The kitchen became the headquarters for the deadly game of hide-and-seek. It filled with men made larger than life in their overclothes, men with serious faces that were red and dripping with melting ice after their lashing by the weather outside. They sectored the settlement in groups of twos and threes, and when, after three hours, there was still no sign of the mother and her son, opinions as to the outcome split into two camps.

"She's perished, he's perished, they're gone," said one. "No mortal can stay alive out on a night such as this."

"The little woman's got sense," said the other. "They'll make a hole in the snow and bide till the breeze pitches back."

The unspoken worry of all concerned is that the two took the wrong trail early on, the one that leads to the harbour and over the new ice. They would never get out of the freezing water on such a night.

They were found just after midnight, alive and looking amazingly well after their six-hour ordeal. They had gone more than half a mile from the settlement, and then, realizing they were hopelessly lost, had sensibly holed up.

Later I heard that an American volunteer teacher had died in the same storm, fifty miles up the shore in Quebec. He had ignored advice against taking a walk to try out his new snowshoes and had not known the laws of survival, the avoidance of exposure.

Lourdes-de-Blanc-Sablon

There was a pathetic incident today. I found myself in a small side room at the hospital with two nuns and a small rough coffin of unpainted spruce. The nuns and I were searching in our pockets for a dime or a nickel to use to open the screws of the coffin lid. Inside was the corpse of a girl of three years, drowned two days ago after being swept under the ice of a partly opened brook. She had been dressed in her best white frock and looked unnaturally alive, like a big, expensive doll. The weather has been down for two days, and they had to wait before they could get her here for the death certificate.

Castors River

The sight of a few blades of long grass beside an open brook made me stop the jeep and do an improvised jig on the road. I provided my own music. Two little girls playing house in an upturned boat near Castors River saw me. The winter is over! I could hardly believe the world was still there under the snow. The dance was quite spontaneous – I was out of the door before I knew what I was doing, two skid marks on the road. It was lucky there was no one behind me – it would have been hard to explain to a man whose head I had put through his windscreen. I did not know I was finding the winter so burdensome. Maybe it's because the cold always needs an effort to overcome, even if one's not conscious of it, and that levies a tax on energy. It's as though memory is short, and I had forgotten there was a land without the ice age, and that meadows with loose, waving grass and running water and blue sea were normal things to see.

Winter certainly dominates the year. Like many dictatorships it begins quietly and catches us unawares sometime in early January, and by this time it is even too late to get away; the inshore water will not allow a boat to pass, and the ice will not bear up an aircraft.

There was one death that affected me more personally than all the others. Bob Russell from Rexons Cove, who was my dog team driver on the first trip I ever made, was drowned in the late winter of 1970. He was travelling home, alone at night, from Port Hope Simpson, and drove his skidoo over thin ice, which parted under him. The next day searchers from Rexons Cove found a large, open stretch of water, and it was thought probable that he had struggled in the water for hours, beating at the edge of the ice that broke continually under him. They found his over trousers on the ice and thought he had taken them off to be more mobile in his unsuccessful fight for life. Stanley Campbell from Pinsent's Arm and some other men from his settlement laid long sticks of wood on the ice to support themselves, and pulled the body from the water after snaring it in jigging hooks.

A grisly postscript to Bob's death was that his body, which was taken away to Goose Bay for an autopsy, was returned several days later, but to the wrong settlement. A police airplane landed in Charlottetown, which is not far from Rexons Cove, and the pilot, worried about the lateness of the day and the deteriorating weather situation, left the body, tied up in a sack, on the ice of the bay. A man, realizing what had happened, put the sack into his shed for the night before Bob's relatives could collect it.

Lastly, there is the story of a lady who had died at an advanced old age from natural causes. She was being brought from one settlement to another, where the soil was deep enough to dig a grave, and the komatik carrying her coffin went over a small cliff. The coffin came adrift and smashed open, and, as was told at the funeral, which was not much delayed, "Aunt Elsie was a little late coming because she burst abroad on the way."

In all I was directly acquainted with ten people who subsequently died as a result of accidents. Although doctors see more of death than most, and of course I saw my share of people dying as a result of illness, I was not professionally involved with any of the ten I mentioned above. It is true that I was on the move all the time, and perhaps met more people than most, but the number was still a large one. It bolsters the statistics.

LIFE AND DEATH AND
THE USE OF DOGS

A doctor is more often a witness to events than the agent of altering their course. This is especially true in the case of birth and death, and the medical rituals performed on these occasions are more to soothe the congregation than to do anything else. Most births and deaths are, after all, natural and normal. But too many of them can wear one down.

These were thoughts flitting round a tired head as I sat in the airplane with a sleepless night behind me, and although I did not know it, most of the next night would also be sleepless. I was leaving Blanc Sablon, a hospital in Northern Quebec to which I was occasionally lent to do locum tenens, and in my last few hours in the place I had left its population three greater than before. Twins compound the complications of childbirth and, to an extremely amateur obstetrician like myself, fan the flames of possibly groundless worries. The mother was an Indian woman who spoke neither French nor English. The twins had not been diagnosed until the second one came instead of the afterbirth, and even her labour almost went unnoticed because we were busy with another woman who had arrived by skidoo and komatik from a snowdrift between her community and the hospital, with her baby half born.

Although I did not know it at the time I was on my way to a death, as if nature was to settle her account for the new additions of the morning. In the back of the little aircraft, with my bag on my knee, I looked over the snow-covered forests, seemingly as flat and featureless as pack ice, watching the low sun glinting on the occasionally bare ice of uncovered ponds. We saw a moose and went down for a better look, but did not land because we had patients with us. Five minutes later we were landing on a pond near one of the communities on the northeast Newfoundland coast, the broad skis of the aircraft slapping on the ribbed snow, and I was met by a man with an old skidoo, old, oily clothes, and a ragged fur hat and patched skin boots. He had no teeth, which made him look old at first glance, but his eyes were blue and razor sharp and his expression keen. It was too frosty to do more than smile and nod, clamber onto his machine that was more improvised spare parts than original, and be off. He made the sign of the Cross as we began the descent down the precipitous trail to the houses.

The Catholic communities had a different atmosphere to their Protestant neighbours. They had often been established longer, and the architecture of the houses was subtly different, as if they had been constructed by shipwrights, more curved, more evidence of old timber. It was a reminder of history that the Protestant communities often lacked, and the people in them showed a unity in the common denominators of ritual and custom, and in their obvious ties with Rome. Most medical emergencies were more a cause for a sprint to the priest's home before ever the nurse was considered.

The knowledge that Uncle Joseph Mary McGrath was feeling a "bit quare" filtered through to me during the short clinic I did in the house of the man who met me at the pond. I had not known that most of the community was away at a wedding down the shore, gone with the priest and a komatik load of moonshine, and the clinic consisted of one child and his grandmother. After this, it was a hearty lunch and the afternoon was dissolved in talk. It was getting dark when I walked up the track over the hard-packed snow to the house where Joseph Mary lived with his son. The path to the kitchen door passed over the tips of a paling fence that encircled the house, set away from the others, and the tips of the fence threw long shadows over the snow. The yellow light, laced with swirls of tobacco smoke, was coming from the open door, which was filled with a scrum of old men, peering indoors over each other's shoulders.

"It's the doctor, let him through, will ya?" I pushed through the crowd, who were only outside because there was no room for them in the kitchen.

"'Tis not the doctor we're wanting," said Joseph Mary's son. "It's more of a priest could be any use tonight."

The patient was at once obvious in the gathering, standing head and shoulders above everyone else, his great head on one side, massive and concentrating, grey hair falling over his face, looking for all the world like a respected poet giving a recital of his work to a rather unlikely audience.

"Could we clear the kitchen?" I asked, always the first thing to do. "Perhaps only his close relatives would stay behind." No one moved. It was true – they probably were all close relatives. I tried another tack. "Give a man some room, will you, or you'll get the needle by mistake."

"You're no use to me," said Joseph Mary, "unless you've bringed your shovel along. I'm finished."

The room was cleared a little and, possibly now that my presence had registered, there was a shy silence about. A young woman wearing an apron and with snow still on her slippers was sitting and weeping. Joseph Mary, whose great, square face was showing signs of all the strange things going on in his head, looked at the girl, then concentrated on her.

"Light the candle, maid, light the candle for Jasus' sake."

As he spoke his right hand fell limp, dropping a piece of rag to the floor, and his body slipped to the right as the stroke took the strength from his right leg, but miraculously he did not fall. The right side of his face wilted until the mouth sloped parallel to his drooping moustache. His expression registered a losing fight with reason; he was like the biggest of the icebergs at the breathless moment before it toppled.

"Light the candle, maid." We could barely make out the words, but they whipped the room into action. Someone was stuffing a candle into his good hand, and another plunging a spill of paper into the stove to light it. Joseph Mary had had the last rites from several priests goodness knows how many times, but tonight it looked like he was dying for real and the good father was off boozing at the wedding. It is dangerous and expensive to die without the last rites. The soul lacks the credentials to get to heaven, and several Masses have to be paid for to put the soul on its way. But as it is in many seemingly hopeless situations, there are loopholes, and in this case, it was provided by a lit candle, which seemed to function as a hastily improvised travel permit. Even in this scrambled situation it was a moving gesture, full of effective symbolism.

Joseph Mary was saved from dying standing up. It took three men to get him sitting on the hard, wooden daybed. He looked at me, laughing with helplessness, groping for my arm with his sinewy, blotched hand. An ironical, mirthless laugh was all that was left to him. The laugh was more expressive than anything he could have said.

Two men, still in their thick outdoor clothes, were mixing Carnation milk from a tin with a good measure of rum. They broke an egg into it. There were tea leaves floating on the top because they were in the cup to begin with. The drink was applied to Joseph Mary's gargoyle mouth, and some flowed in, causing him to choke; the rest formed rivulets in the creases of his jowls and neck, and dripping onto the lapels of his coat.

He lay back, gripping the candle with a slight tremor that made our shadows dance on the walls like conspirators. I stayed there with three other men, his two brothers and his son, until his breathing stopped. After a while all sense of emergency passed, and it seemed normal to wait for the man to die. I sat and looked at the candle, and wondered about the twins of the morning, and thought that it can be easy to die after all.

The adrenaline had stopped pumping and was flowing into visceral backwaters, lapping insistently. Urgency was spreading itself thinly through the day, diluted and made less urgent by the hours that passed. The day was fine, although we were in a clear arena ranked by low cloud that had prevented an aircraft from flying in. The dogs went at their own pace, which had to suffice for us.

I am possibly the last person ever to have gone on a medical emergency by dog team, and however vicariously diverting, it was a severe test of patience. I am sure that the few other individuals who have been through the experience would not choose to repeat it, and that is doubly sure for the patient. A woman in obstructive labour would be bumped off to hospital in more ways than one by dog team, and nowadays, in the frozen Labrador winter, it is proper that she should listen for the sound of an approaching aircraft rather than the yelping of eight dogs.

If I had been more cold-blooded about the situation I would have shot the dogs and pushed their anachronistic carcasses through a hole in the ice. I would not have argued so hard to keep the winter trips going. It cost twenty-five dollars a day for the hire of two teams, and the administrators, who had to provide the money, reckoned that with the twentieth century three quarters gone there were more vital projects for their budget.

Looking back, the fervour of my first brushes with the boss was so tinged with romanticism that I blush to think of it. I wanted to go, that's all, to see what it was really like; it was one of the reasons why I had left England in the first place. I pretended to understand what I was told: that a doctor and a nurse could have seen the same number of patients, prescribed the same number of drugs, carried out the same number of procedures (or however else medical productivity could be quantified) on a series of flying trips by bush aircraft, in less than half the time it took travelling by dogs. The Royal Canadian Mounted Police made their last official beat by dog team in 1970, and our parson zoomed by on a twenty-five horsepower snowmobile, racing the welfare officer and the fur buyer on their skidoos. No one with serious business travel used dogs any more.

Yet in retrospect the arguments I pulled so magically from

my fur hat do make sense. Dogs, like nothing else invented (certainly not the fickle internal combustion engine), do not have spark plug trouble or burnt-out magnetos, are not grounded in dirty weather, never need transplant surgery – costly spare parts – or imported fuel, and, not least, provide a safety margin if things go wrong. Unlike skidoos, they reproduce themselves. With more sophistication than a lunar module, they will find their way home if the going gets really rough, and even provide warmth if it is so rough that it is better to hole up. I know three people, one of whom is Bob Russell, who perished by drowning after falling through bad ice on skidoos. With dog teams it is probable they would be alive today; dogs sense thin or rotten ice. Dogs are better, too, in soft going, where the heavier, compact mechanical sleds sink a foot or more into the slushy snow, and they can pull the greater payloads that the medical trips need, especially over hilly ground.

Dogs have a definite exhaust smell, especially after a feed of seal meat and fish heads, but it is nothing to the noise and fumes from the two-stroke engine of a skidoo, that can give a thudding headache, and, even though the journey is half or a quarter of the time, put one in no mood to work at the end of it. It does no harm to experience the day without pushing the pace, if some of the day's work can be displaced into the evening. And in bad conditions we kept on the move, not kicking our heels listening to gloomy forecasts, dependent on an aircraft and the changeable weather. We were able to stay in communities overnight, and in the larger ones for several days, and get to know people. The children saw us get up in the mornings, wash our faces and eat our breakfast like normal human beings, and stopped being frightened of us. We had spare time to visit the bedridden and the elderly – who on flying visits often were ignored – and we talked to people about other things besides medicine and what troubled them. Travelling with the dogs enabled us to have more balanced relationships with people.

Dogs helped open up the country, in so far as Southern Labrador could be said to be opened up. At least they made it possible for people to be mobile in the winter, a season that spanned almost six months, on paths that closed behind them as they went, to haul loads of wood for fires and timber for building boats and homes.

But in the summer months they had no use at all and had to be fed and cared for until the coming of the ice made travel possible again. Between May and December they were either staked out and chained in the mud and dust, often with shelter from a hut or under a house, or they were let loose to roam free and forage for themselves. If there was an island near the summer settlement, they were occasionally marooned on it until the next winter, squabbling over the flotsam for their food and greeting each boat that passed with a snarling chorus.

If the dogs were free for the summer, they would roam

in packs, with six months to forget the laws of man, to align themselves with one side of their schizoid natures, that of mob rule and aggressive wildness. There was a delinquent psychopath in every dog, although balanced in each of them by charm and enthusiasm for work. The many acts of savagery that resulted from this summer redundancy was the main reason why most people on the coast were not sorry to see the last of the dogs. With about fifteen teams to a settlement of three hundred people – about a hundred and fifty dogs counting the pups and breeding bitches, and all kept half wild by the natural history of their condition – it is no wonder that mothers kept a watchful eye on their children. In 1970, to my knowledge, three people died as a result of being savaged by dogs, but the number is small compared to past history.

To look after a team of dogs is hard work. They bicker and grumble, fall sick, and injure themselves. They howl at the moon and need hushing in the early hours. They need feeding every day and seal carcasses are often scarce. They have to be trained and need to be kept in training by being spliced to harnesses and pulling komatiks. Out of all the details and methodology of travelling by dog team, a system of culture and folklore has grown up which will have disappeared in the near future, when the takeover by skidoo is complete. The special word usages and ways of doing things, the knots in the tackle and harsh words of command, the skills of choosing a leader for the team and the choice of a trail, like the traditions of the sailing ships of the past, are not being handed on as living culture; nor, unlike the ways of the sea, will they be recorded in detail, because they are not the product of such universal medium. They come from a shy, hidden part of the world, and are in the process of passing, unlamented by most.

A young dog is put into his traces for the first time when he is a little over a year old. It is a rough apprenticeship. The unaccustomed harness is on, and suddenly, for no apparent reason the team is off, leaving him behind, dragging in the snow, tail under the komatik runners, yelping, somersaulting, throttled, booted in the face, and jumped on. He has never known violence like this before; yesterday he was a pup, sleeping free in the wood shavings where Freeman is building a boat. The man threatens to shoot him, like he shot Tobe yesterday in front of Aunt Dorcas's house, calls him a godawful-mortal-bastard-son-of-a-christless-bitch, and kicks him in the balls. The dog gets the idea and runs awkwardly behind Old Watch, and in the deep snow he would have avoided yesterday he has to jump up and down, lacking Watch's great shoulders for barging through. He falls behind, and the runners are on his tail again, the trace is caught tightly around his haunches, and the man kicks his head, blood flowing into his eyes, jumps on top of him, and embeds him in the snow. After two days of this sort of treatment, and nights spent sleeping exhausted in the snow, staked and chained where before he was free, he finds breath comes more easily, and as well as keeping up with the rest of the team he has energy to pull. He is promoted in line, enjoying the day, and Watch is two behind him. Watch is old, his father's father, and will be the next to be shot.

The dogs each had their own trace, made those days of half-inch nylon rope, which led from their harness to a loop of warp between the upcurved front end of the komatik runners. Each trace was of a different length, the leader's the longest at about ten yards, so that animals could run in a single line through the woods and along the trails, and yet fan out on the bays and ponds. The harnesses were made of a softer, natural fibre rope, spliced to make three loops, one for the head and one for each front leg and shoulder, so that the strain of pulling was taken at the front end of the dog. The trace was attached to the join in the loops over the animal's back. In spite of its softness, which was further softened by binding and covering it with sackcloth, at the end of the winter each dog had the shape of its harness chafed into bald markings on its back and flanks.

The komatik, one of several Labrador terms on loan from the Inuit, is a simple construction of two runners made with planks of wood on edge, planed up to a curve at their forward ends, with the curve continued up nine or so inches with the addition of two small pieces of wood. The running surfaces are fashioned with a metal strip. Between the runners are placed planks of spruce wood, traditionally lashed in place with cord or sealskin thongs; contemporary ones are more often nailed.

Onto this komatik platform, which is about thirty inches wide, the boxes were tied, the driver's box containing his axe, a hammer and nails for running repairs, some food wrapped up in a cloth, matches, tobacco and some bottles of beer, and our boxes with the patients' notes, medical supplies, instruments, and our personal necessities. A loaded box weighed about fifty pounds, and each team had at least three of them to haul, as well as the driver and his passenger. The box provided the seats, and the edges and corners of the komatik somewhere to place one's feet between the snowshoes, the gun, and the spare rope and chains for staking out the dogs in strange settlements. The area of bare perch on the boxes was further eroded by a rucksack and a sleeping bag, a small crate of pills and potions, badges, ophthalmoscope, sphygmomanometer, plaster of Paris bandages, lumbar puncture apparatus, bottle of ether and a mask for administering it, syringes, vaccines; we take everything, sometimes including a sort of kitchen sink, a galvanized tub for carrying, preparing, and serving the dog's food.

The dogs ate once a day, in the evening, and their menu was made up of seal carcasses, meal, fish heads and scraps, stirred into a soup du jour with hot water. Although the animals appeared indestructible, their stamina was dependent on the correct fuel, and this had to be carefully chosen, taking into account the nature of the land ahead, the degree of frost, the depth and firmness of the snow, and the state of the trails.

All this information is contained in the word "footing." The consistency of the dogs' feces was also important. Too much grease in their food gave them diarrhea, which sapped their forces and slowed them down; insufficient grease deprived them of energy in the cold weather. The balance of fat and the state of the footing were matters of earnest discussion among the drivers each evening.

The dogs themselves were not of pure husky breed, although they had husky characteristics: wide, grinning faces, curly raised tails, squat stance and broad shoulders, and quick, vicious tempers. They were big dogs, standing over twenty-four inches high at the shoulder, and they trotted and loped on hefty paws more than three inches across. All in all they were better as friends than enemies. They looked very much like the wolves of the forest, whose blood and ancestry they shared, and who were to be seen every now and again, alone on the bay in the distance, or else close at hand, as corpses, and pelts offered for sale. The team dogs were never pets at any stage in their hard lives. Dogs that were allowed into the house were not even called or thought of as dogs, but known as "crackies."

Our teams came from Rexons Cove in the south of Labrador, one of the few communities that had continued through choice with the traditional way of life.

Our "blind message" over the transmitter in the nursing station, telling Rexons Cove that we were ready to travel, would have been received on the wireless sets tuned to our frequency in the kitchens of each of the eight homes in the community. The medical trips had involved Rexons Cove for many years, and the trustful way we released our abstract pigeon into the ether would be rewarded that night with the arrival of teams in Mary's Harbour. Perhaps there had been two or three sentences spoken by the nurse to the Rexons Cove people in connection with the impending medical trips, and these a month or two previously, before freeze-up; even then it would have been more in the nature of hints rather than definite intentions, but traditions and reliability were strong corpuscles in the blood of these people. I had never seen such nebulous arrangements kept so faithfully before or since.

The message was sent on January 15, 1970, as a spell of fine weather drifted over Labrador. The etiquette of transmitting procedure emptied it of any personality or friendliness, but the words had an odd ring for modern times.

"This is Mary's Harbour. Mary's Harbour with a message for Mr. Leonard Russell, to say that the nurse and a doctor are ready to travel and will be needing two teams. End of message."

The imperative nature of this summons was neutralized by our isolated situation, by the absence of telephones, and by the willingness with which the Rexons Cove men participated in the winter trips. Unless they were house or boat building, they were more than glad to be the ones chosen by Uncle Len to "haul the doctor," exercising the working dogs, visiting relations, friends, and women in other settlements, and enjoying a break from the closed-circuit atmosphere of a small Labrador outport in the winter. The early deference of the men went in the first day or so, and any possible relationship of the master-and-servant type was soon transcended by mutual willingness. In any case, it would have been a facade impossible to maintain, perched with one man all day on the komatik box, dependent on him in very hard conditions for protection, knowledge, and company.

The teams arrived the same evening, and we left the following morning, walking from the nursing station over the harbour ice in our bulky travelling clothes to the house of George Snook, Uncle Len's son-in-law, where the drivers had spent the night. Hughlett Acreman, the nursing station foreman, had taken the boxes over before us by skidoo, and the men were lashing them onto the komatiks.

All about us the dogs were prowling, seventeen of them, becoming excited by degrees, barking and yelping, stretching and yawning as expressions of the tension. With sudden violence they dug frantically into the crusty snow, then snapped up the bloody ice when it cut their paws. Old enemies met and strutted stiff-legged in parallel, hackles up, growling their threats. On the mounting tempo, the komatiks were dragged by all of us from outside the house, down the slope of the foreshore onto the harbour ice, and wedged behind a hillock of ice which had been rafted up by the tides. Then we went and got the dogs, who allowed themselves to be caught with dignity, except for one, Uncle Len's pup, and put them into their harnesses, standing astride the temporarily cowed animals. One of them snarled, showed her curved white teeth, head on one side, neck exposed and vulnerable, already defeated in the act of defiance. She was booted hard on the nose, and her jaw was dislocated for a few seconds, a gesture, by the way, which set the scene of the relationship.

One saw at first only violence, the well-aimed kicks, the harsh language, the specific and oft carried out threats, the blood, the murderous day's work. But after some time the violence passed from the realms of cruelty to the natural enforcement of discipline. It was not that sensibilities were dulled by repetition, but rather that harshness was seen in the context of what had to be done. The dogs themselves, whose individual personalities became obvious as the first day passed, were paradoxically the agents of my change of heart; they showed no resentment of violence when it was part of the normal pattern of the day. They did not cower when all was going well and did not hoard malice like maltreated animals. It was obvious, from their enthusiasm to be off in the mornings, from the jaunty way they reacted to praise when the going was good, and their excellent physical health, that they had a symbiotic relationship with man. Coming from a pet-orientated culture, it is difficult for me to describe the dogs and their possible motivation without an orgy of empathy; the Labrador man had no such difficulty. Yet the stories of cruel men eaten by abused dogs were told with the same relish and moral attitudes adopted by the societies of prevention of cruelty and they were said to have deserved their fate.

In groups of two and three, rushing forward at the end of their traces, almost toppling the man holding them, the dogs were taken down to the harbour. The traces were tied with a sheet bent onto the sliced loop of warp between the runners of the wedged komatik, and each dog had to be held back by several men to give enough slack for the knot to be tied. Our help had come from a crowd who had collected from neighbouring houses to chat and give a hand, people to whom travelling by dog team was nothing new. The doctor in his fur hat was today's curiosity.

The excitement of the dogs was frenzied as they fanned out in front of the komatiks, straining forward and jumping high with a springing four-legged takeoff, some dancing on their hind legs, howling and yelping. A boy had managed to catch Uncle Len's pup, and while he was harnessed up, we untangled our traces, which had become entwined halfway down when the third dog jumped over the backs of the others and returned to his position by crawling underneath them. I sat on the komatik, sweating with the effort in my thick clothes and taking in the brisk scene of the harbour ice. To the east, beyond the ice edge in the Atlantic, the crystal of the morning sky was marred by a scoop of rapidly gathering wisps of cirrus.

Then the komatik was freed with a shove from its

obstructing pillar of ice. There was a jerk forward, a bucking acceleration as we rode the lump of ice, and we were hissing along at a steady speed, the harbour miraculously silent, the barking, the yapping, cursing melee transformed into a smooth, magical movement forward. The new sounds breaking into the silence were the panting of eight dogs, the pattering crunch of their paws in the snow, and the creaking of the komatik and its articulated load as it slipped over the tracked snow of the harbour. The driver in front of me was chucking to the dogs, soft wet clicks of sound between his tongue and the roof of his mouth, and their ears pricked up. He called their names in a thudding, abrupt way, and as the roll call went on each dog reacted in its turn by straining forward, tightening its trace. I learned the names from the leader's back: Spot, Tiger, Ring, Fly, Eilich, Watch, Scout, Breeze.

Len Russell, who was driving the other team with the nurse, was calling to his dogs in a harsher, scolding way, and he caught up to us, then steadied to our pace, his voice losing its rasp. He put up his jacket hood and blew his nose in the lee of it, then folded his handkerchief carefully and rolled and lit a cigarette. I saw him pointing at the clouds gathering to the east and saying something to the nurse, and she nodded to him and shrugged her shoulders. I watched her shift her position on the box, automatically leaning as the komatik rolled and pitched on the rough ice, pulling on her thick pair of overgloves. Margaret Harris had been in Mary's Harbour for seven years, and I calculate that she had travelled more than three thousand miles by dog team in that time; not, in fact, all that unusual an accomplishment for a girl from Weston Super Mare. After all, the West Country of England over the centuries had provided much of the Labrador stock.

Uncle Len had "hauled" her nearly every one of those three thousand miles. He was universally respected on the coast, a deceptively mild man, starting to become old then with the beginning of a stoop and watery edges to his eyes. Most societies produce men and women who lead exemplary lives, people with natural status who are looked up to, with no tag of conceit pinned on them, and Uncle Len was one of these. He had also the extra facets of the pioneer – self-reliance, providence, and the ability to assess physical danger – which was a product of his special environment in the harsh Labrador, although he would have been the first to ridicule the idea.

Margaret had dropped one of her gloves, but Uncle Len made no attempt to stop the team. At this early stage of the day it would have taken a hundred yards, a gallon of sweat, and a dictionary of blasphemy to bring eight dogs to a halt. Someone with a skidoo might find the glove and catch up to us. Uncle Len's leader, Nanuk, was trotting fast, his head six inches from my left knee. His acceleration had been slowed by us, and now as his trace slackened, the second dog came to dispute his place. As they ran there was a fracas involving the third dog as well, ground was lost, and amid an angry bellow from Len there was a frantic assertion of place as they strained to catch us again.

"Uncle Len's a wonderful hand for shootin' dogs," said Bob, my driver, as we detached ourselves from the settlement past the last few houses. There was all day ahead of us, and as we got to know each other there was enough to talk about. Bob was about my age, about my build. He called me Doctor. He told me the footing was soft and dusty on the bays when they came from Rexons Cove yesterday, but the neck of land was good. The dogs had not been long in their traces that year, hadn't yet found their wind, and it had been a hard day.

The cirrus in the eastern sky was packing a skein around the sun and a breeze was springing up in our faces. The dogs were in single file, jostling after the leader between the trees on a neck of land between two long ponds. The path split in two, and the leader chose the left turn without a word from Bob.

"Spot, you bastard," said Bob, as encouragement. Spot was a good leader, retracing her steps of yesterday, on firm snow that lay under the surface powder, packed by previous traffic. There was a hill down to the next pond and Bob used a loop of chain, called a drug, which he threw over one of the komatik runners to slow us down. On the hill, which becomes steep, there was a curve, and we used our legs to steer the accelerating craft, altering course with our feet in the deep side snow, lying sideways on the box. In spite of the drug we lost control for ten or more seconds, flying and bouncing, snow in our faces, catching up with the dogs. We actually ran over the slowest one, pressing him into the snow until he emerged behind, dragging along, screaming with fright. Then another curve and a larger boulder beside it, and lying horizontally on the box I ran along it, fending us off. Bob kneeled on the platform in front of the boxes, gripping the runners, leaning forward beyond the cloud of powdery snow like a figurehead ahead of a ship's spray, and at the whim of gravity we careened onto flatter ground and rescued the three-quarters throttled dog.

The commands for turning left and right are supposed to have their origins in the language of the Inuit. Right is yuk or uk, spoken with a grunt, repetitively, until the leader has changed course by the required angle. Then the driver stops his row of yuks, and the leader continues on the new course, followed, it is hoped, by the other dogs. For left the order is an open-throated noise that can be rendered as "hedder," with the "r" at the larynx. Often on the first change of direction the leader would go too far, and have to be brought back with the appropriate "yuk" or "hedder"; again too far, and back the other way, until the hunting word fluctuations produced the right heading. It sounded something like this:

"Spot, Spot, Spot, chuck, chuck, Spot, yuk, yuk, yuk, uk, uk, uk, uk, uk, uk, Spotspotspotspotspotspot, yuk, yuk, uk, hedder, hedder, hedder, hedder, hedder, der, der, der, der, uk, uk, yuk, yuk, YUK, YUK." At this point Bob jumped up and sprinted as fast as he could down the line of dogs, limbs flailing as he slipped on a patch of clear ice and put the boot in.

On our first day of driving dogs the air was full of similar misunderstandings, but the animals were willing, and also susceptible to pain, and at the end of the day they would be going well, with heads and tails up, acutely aware of the whims and wishes of the driver. We left the land and changed course by going onto the sea ice on the first bay. The open sea was to our backs, the edge of the ice two miles behind us, and we stayed on this deep fjord for four hours as we made slow headway into the eye of the wind. Under the surface powder there was a deep, slushy snow, and the dogs were in it up to their shoulders, having to jump to keep to the pitted tracks made by Spot.

For more than two hours Bob walked ahead with snowshoes, beating down the snow for the dogs. I walked with him for less than half an hour with all the grace and effort of an amputee trying on his new legs for the first time. I stopped, fully out of breath, let the komatik catch up with me, and sank onto it; or rather climbed up onto it. Even with rackets I had sunk three feet into the snow, slobby where the tide had seeped over the top of the ice on the bay and turned into slush.

Deeper in the bay the footing was firmer and we made better time. There was a shout; Uncle Len suddenly called for us to stop, and we walked back to him through the dusty surface snow that was beginning to be blown up. One of his dogs had dropped dead. It was the pup we had only managed to catch at the last moment, and in the freezing conditions he was already stiff and brittle, five minutes after his heart stopped beating. I think it was probably subaortic stenosis, but scientific curiosity balked at taking my knife and finding out; Bob said unemotionally, "He lost his wind in the slob and his heart gave out," which came to much the same thing.

The dead animal was stripped of its trace and harness and pushed out of the komatik's way, and we went on to worsening conditions. Swirling clouds of blown surface snow engulfed us in the nothingness of the bay, and the dead pup was the sole point of reference. The small, grey blur of his body, already silted with snow, receded into the close distance and then became confused into the pale shadows. The sky, the horizon, and the earth were all merged; for two hours the only real things in the world were the teams and the huddled people on them. Then I felt the komatik humping over a hard mound of ice, struggled to get my balance at the new angle, saw a tree, and another, and a line of them down the shore of the bay. We left the sea ice and started up a steep trail over the rocks and into the woods, mercifully out of the wind.

Sheltered from the bitter breeze, we cut wood and lit a fire to boil up some snow for tea. Bread was spread with butter by holding the wooden slab of butter in the flames and rubbing it on a slice. Bob cut some fronds of spruce for Margaret to stand on, to insulate her feet from the cold, and the dogs moved off the trail, their traces snaking into the woods either side of us. They slept, almost buried in the snow.

When the clouds had covered the sky, the temperature rose and snow began to fall. We started off again, leaving the land for a long, curving pond. Bob and I sat sideways into the wind, our parka hoods up to hide our faces as the dogs struggled to keep us going at walking pace. He was encouraging them, whistling, cajoling, cursing, calling their names. When we got cold we ran alongside the team, banging our gloves together and swinging our arms; the dogs accepted me, a stranger, without cowering or snarling as they had done at first. I was proud of my acceptance and felt that a companionship had grown between us all that crossed the barriers of culture, even species. It was easier once it was impossible to talk, the breeze whipping our balloons of words up into the swirling sky. The first round of our acquaintance was over and more talk would have had to go over things already said, autobiography and question and answer. Yet it was difficult to keep silent when you were sitting touching the only human being for miles around, and I was glad for this icy involvement in the moment.

We crossed another bay, leaving one shore and lurching over the rocks of the other side and seeing nothing but the whirling snow. Again we warmed up on a long forest trail and then walked beside the dogs on a series of ponds. The strap broke on my left snowshoe and I mended it with the drawstring from one of the sleeping bags. We reached our destination an hour after dark, a blind tumble down a gully to a hidden bay with a settlement of five families. There were paraffin lights in the windows of the unpainted frame houses, and dogs and crackies came barking over the ice to welcome our tired animals.

Our welcome was at Stanley Campbell's house, and we sat around his big kitchen table to eat as soon as we arrived: Margaret Harris, Len and Bob Russell, Stanley and his eldest son, Harrison, while Stanley's wife, Mildred, walked around keeping the table full. Uncle Len said the blessing and we ate bottled spruce partridge, with turnips, potatoes, and bread, followed by cakes and cups of tea.

While the men fed the dogs, we made ready to carry out a clinic in the room next to the kitchen. As we had been eating, people had begun drifting into the kitchen to sit quietly on the daybed and chairs around the wall. According to the division of labour, Margaret checked on two antenatal women and gave triple vaccines to children of four of the families, and I went outside to watch the feeding of the dogs.

Ravenous appetites, especially carnivorous ones, excite me, and judging by the numbers of people who pay good money to get into zoos at feeding time, I am not alone in my fascination. Uncle Len was scooping oatmeal and lumps of margarine into a tub while Bob chopped a cylindrical, skinned seal carcass into sections with an axe, and the sections into pieces half the size of a fist. The frozen meat was added to Uncle Len's mixture, and a gallon of hot water poured over the lot. The brew was stirred with a stick and Uncle Len's dogs hovered outside, an invisible circle, shaking, salivating, gulping, eyes on the tub with taut concentration. One moment the tub and its contents was by itself on the snow in the sprawl of lights from the kitchen window, the next the same area was converted into a sea of fur. The heads were dipped up to the ears in the gore, and there was much snapping and underwater snarling. One dog had a big lump of meat and took it a few yards away, growling a warning to the rest not to take it away from him. He was a big, cream-coloured fellow, but then his whole head was red from dunking. In three minutes the tub was empty with the dogs licking their dessert off each other's heads and necks, and it was the turn of the other team to eat.

Our clinic was a rudimentary affair in terms of lives saved or vital diagnoses made. No one in the settlement was ill except an elderly woman who was dying from cancer and old age, but we checked up on the normality of pregnancies, of which there were two in the settlement at that time, vaccinated the children, tried to explain the worrisome symptoms that most people have from time to time but which were magnified in the isolated situation, and reassured. By the light of a hurricane lamp I fit an intrauterine contraceptive device into a woman of twenty-nine who had eight living children.

The clinic lasted three hours, and after it, rather than use the pail in the semi-privacy of one of the rooms, I went outside to perform natural functions that had been nagging me for some time. As I squatted in the snow on the shore below the house, freezing a little, about twenty dogs, an expanse of fur and cold noses in the pitch dark, crowded fearlessly about me. I called out a few names – Spot, Fly, Ring, chuck, chuck, Breeze – more to reassure myself than anything else, and then they pressed in on me, knocking me over. I ran indoors, pulling up my complicated clothes, aiming kicks and abuse that made contact with nothing in the dark, frosty air.

Emergencies apart, to my mind it was not just a nostalgic indulgence that kept up the tradition of the routine winter medical trips by dog team. Maybe it was the content of my arguments more than my romantically tinged zeal that won the day and kept the trips going in my time, but somehow I doubt it. Anyway, the trips stopped and the last of the dogs were drowned in the spring of 1973.

CHRISTMAS AND NEW YEAR'S EVE

Even illness takes a happy nature at Christmastime; to this day I have sharp memories of a patient in my hospital in London, an elderly man dying of pneumonia in an oxygen tent, smiling through blue lips and with a festive paper hat on his head. Somehow the coming of Christmas adds zest to the routine, and my clinics in Newfoundland were no exception to this.

A few days before Christmas Eve, my travels had taken me to an outport in the north of Newfoundland. It was very cold indeed, and not much snow had fallen, which was unusual for so late in the year. An old woman in the house where the clinic was held (the tip of whose toothless jaw met the end of her nose and who would have been burned as a witch long ago) told me that a green Christmas meant a full graveyard. Mercifully it snowed that very day, and the precursor to the filling of the graveyard, days and nights that would have kept me extremely busy, was avoided. The heavy snowfall also had the effect of stranding me in an outport whose new road gave it only the most tenuous of connections with the outside world.

Because medicine was outside everyone's knowledge and experience, most people thought it must be hard work, and I was approached in a solicitous way and invited to "take a spell." I stayed in a house that could make room for me, three girls vacating their bed and moving in with various relatives, and my presence brought a shy quietness into the household. Children sat, not playing, the old prophetic woman glared at me (although I later discovered she was blind), the man Jack, whose house it was, struck up a half-hearted conversation about "the government," while his wife skinned and cut up a porcupine without saying a word. It was only later on in the evening that things livened up.

When we had eaten the Labrador porcupine and the inevitable spuds and turnips, Jack asked me in a cautious way if I would like to take a drink, a hot drink. I was never allowed to forget that I was a missionary, and that mission, whose credit I used, preached absolute sobriety. Jack hedged his question; I was being given the option of interpreting a "hot" drink as a mug of cocoa. I took the bull by the horns and said a glass of rum would be nice, and watched him delve nimbly in the linen box and come out with a full bottle of London Dock. Two glasses were put on the table and in Newfoundland fashion we poured our own. Jack relaxed and put his legs up on the daybed, and Mary Jane, his woman, began to knit a baby's bonnet, using light-blue wool. The children played with live .303 ammunition on the floor and the old blind woman continued glaring at me, then she started to snore and I wondered if she could be asleep.

I had been in Newfoundland long enough to know that no one ever knocks on a door; doors are there to keep out the weather, not people. So that when someone knocked on Jack's door (it was more like someone banging with the side of a fist) everyone in the room stiffened and froze into silence. Jack spilled his drink. After all, everyone in the outport was related and had been through Jack's door a thousand times without knocking. In that isolated place there was suddenly real fear in the room.

"Open up this Jesus door," said a man outside with a peculiar, strangled voice.

"We come to get you, Mary Jane," said a voice made on an in-breath, which then whooped.

"I's the b'y that builds the boat," sang another, a perfect counter-tenor.

"Open up the Jesus door and let the mummers in," said the first voice, then they pushed the door in themselves.

Mary Jane and Jack relaxed, although still looking apprehensive. I was flabbergasted by what I saw coming through the door: three misshapen figures, one carrying a lantern, fell into the room like chained specimens from Bedlam. Two of them were in elaborate "drag," well padded at the bottoms and bosoms, with tatty millinery and scarves hiding their faces. The third – man or woman – was in a sack, with holes cut out for the arms, legs, and eyes, and the top tied over the head.

The harpy in the sack began a sprightly step dance to a jig provided by a fourth man with an accordion who came in behind the mummers.

"That's Charley in the sack, sure," said Mary Jane. "Certainly I'd know him by his step anywhere. Charley, ain't you roastin' in the sack?"

"He's got Lloyd's boots on. Charley's feet's too big for Lloyd's boots. I says it's Freeman. Untie the sack and give us a song, Free."

"Aunt Ethel, Aunt Ethel, I sees you tappin' your toes. Stand up and let's see you step out," said one of the mummers, in falsetto, to the blind old lady.

"That's Bill's young feller," said the old woman, correctly as it turned out. "I never did dance with your father, and I ain't gonna start with you."

Mary Jane had been gathered up into a swirling dance by the larger of the "female" mummers. She kept trying to grab him by the prosthetic parts of his anatomy, the whole room shrieking with delight when his left bosom came adrift, and Mary Jane howling louder than us all when he caught her a thwack across her hindquarters. The company had swelled to about twenty people, and I saw Jack had somehow effected the disappearance of the rum bottle just as nimbly as he had produced it. The dancing mummer was suddenly unmasked in brutal fashion by a sturdy girl who had waltzed up to him in an innocent way. He fought wildly, as if for the virtue implicit in his grotesque disguise, and, as the overhanging scarf came away, and people realized that they had been taken in by him, there was a roar of approval.

I had a sudden glimpse of the whites of the eyes of the man in the sack as he glanced over his non-existent shoulder, looking furtive as only a man in a sack can look. He sidled to the door, still dancing, an egg on legs, and made good his escape before the fate of the mummer in drag overtook him, too. There were several houses still to visit that night, to frighten with the knock on the door and the proximity of a surrogate stranger. The man in the sack was an institution in the community; no one ever found out who he was.

A man smoking a thin cigarette and rolling another was talking to me as I took in the sudden burst of life in Jack's kitchen. He was telling me (without much apparent hope that I was interested or even listening) about the medical problems of some of his older relatives, many of whom had been "given up fer dead" by my predecessors, but had survived only to die of something worse. For him, the visitation by the mummers was, it seemed, as routine as the first snowfall, and he was politely trying to make my evening interesting with snippets and anecdotes of a medical flavour.

But I was snatched away by the sturdy girl (who had a squint that gave her face an out-of-focus, slightly lustful expression).

Encouraged by the evident delight of the audience, I danced my version of a hornpipe, varying it with pseudo cancan and some abandoned skipping, and, as I twirled the girl about the room, she gripped parts of me with the same violence that had been necessary to unmask the mummer. I was a little worried about the implications of the dance, because the same afternoon I had fitted an intrauterine contraceptive device into the same sturdy girl, who already had two illegitimate children, and I suddenly wondered if this was how she was beginning her new life of sexual freedom. However, at the end of the dance, she rushed over to a man in a woolly hat and a big overcoat, who had a bewildered, depressive look about him, and threw her arms around his neck. It was not only the mummers who were unpredictable.

The most frightening of the antics to everyone in the room was that of the last mummer, laughing nervously and, in some cases, hysterically loud; and, when he came near, they recoiled to avoid his touch. His pantomime disguise obviously gave him a licence to terrorize the roomful of willing people. The impoverished costume of borrowed frock, another man's seal boots, padding – to give him a hump at the shoulders and elsewhere to imitate a woman's shape – and tablecloth to hide his face conjured away his personality, converting him into a real stranger, and outside the pale of normal behaviour. For his part he seemed to be free from convention, able to act out fantasies that would normally be taboo. He put his arms around other men's wives and kissed their daughters, whispered obscene suggestions into their ears, and acted mad. He left for another house and I never discovered who he was.

I followed him out of doors and stood in the deep, untrodden snow, watching him trudging into the darkness, chuckling and holding his skirts high. The crowd, Jack included, followed him to watch the fun, leaving me alone with Orion and the Great Bear, dazzling jewels in a black velvet sky. After the sudden madness, the familiar constellations were comforting, but they made me very aware of the isolation of the place I was in. I stood outside for a long time, listening to the sounds of the night: snow slipping in powdery lumps from the roofs, dogs bickering, and the sea lapping on the icy shores, all mixed with the shrill cavorting of the mummers.

The sudden snowfall that had given me the chance to meet the mummers was followed by a very cold spell over Christmas. It took us all by surprise, but none more than the captain of the wood boat – a freighter that had come from Europe to pick up pulpwood from the Newfoundland lumber forests – who found that his ship had stuck fast in the ice. In the provident way that everything in the northern outports is put to some use, our lives became for a while interwoven with the wood ship and all who were stranded in her.

Our relationship began on New Year's Eve, when three healthy-looking seamen came to the nursing station, ostensibly for advice on minor ailments but really to have a look at the nurses. I became involved with one of them, the drunkest, who slipped on the trail from the wharf and sprained his left ankle. The first officer came over to see why I had put the man's leg into a plaster cast, and after about five minutes we found we both used to drink in the same pub in the East India Docks of London – where I had been a house surgeon – and that we knew a lot of people in common. Later, the second officer was dispatched from the ship to say that the "Old Man" had invited us to a Hogmanay party on the ship later that night. The appearance of the second officer, who had the physique of a shot putter, gave me an idea. Ever since a visit I had made earlier in the day, it was clear that we had a problem, and now I had thought of a way in which the sailors of the wood ship could help us solve it.

The house we had visited earlier contained the largest woman I had ever seen in my life, probably the largest I shall ever see. She fully occupied a sagging, brass double bed that itself was the width of the bedroom floor; she had it fitted to suit the bedroom. She was a young woman, about thirty-two, she said, but age was immaterial to her bulk. It was as if she were a different species. Her thighs were so fat that her legs were permanently apart, pushed out to sixty degrees of each other, and for the same reason her arms were away from her body. She lacked any visible neck, only ruffle-like chins, like a pagoda roof, reaching down to her shoulders, and her features were distorted by rounded pads that pressed in on each other. She was a captive on her back, unable to roll over, almost incapable of reaching her mouth with a hand, and she now had pneumonia.

In the house, which was poor but tidy, lived her six children, all boys between the ages of five and fourteen. Skinny and bright-eyed, they stared silently at me, and it seemed odd to think they were of the same flesh and blood as their mother. The family was like the helpless queen bee and her workers. Their father was dead, and his early death had driven his wife to eat compulsively, producing in four years the helpless human mound that confronted me.

The window was heavily curtained with a sacking material and she insisted we leave it so. No one must know of her condition, no one must see her. She was hideous and shameful. I examined her as I would have examined a small whale, kneeling beside her on the narrow ledge of the bed, almost having to crawl over to get to the other side. I guessed she weighed more than four hundred pounds. With the nurses trying to support her, I listened to her lungs at the back, but she fell back, trapping my arm and the stethoscope. We had to find help to lift her and get her to the nursing station in order to try and treat her pneumonia and then put her on a diet; since she refused to let anyone in the community see her, we had a problem, until I thought of the crew of the wood ship.

She would have to be carried because she could not walk:

the fat of her thighs sheathed her lower legs beyond the feet, like a folded telescope. Moreover, a heavy person, particularly an almost spherical one, is a difficult object to lift. I thought we would need four sailors, and after much persuasion she consented to the plan.

Four hefty boys from the ship carried out the operation in a serious and streamlined manner, as if they were taking an injured man off a ship at sea. They had improvised a stretcher about three feet wide, but even so, she hung off at either side, so that one of the boys bruised his arm getting through the door. We put her on a mattress in the back of an open truck and covered her with blankets. When we arrived at the nursing station I thought that she was dead, but it was only the fat cushioning very shallow breathing, and, when I next saw her, propped up in a bed, apparently comfortable and reading a tattered copy of *True Romance* from the station's library, she looked less grotesque.

The only other in-patient at the nursing station was a woman about to give birth to her thirteenth child, in medical parlance a great, grand multip (multiplier), to whom labour pains were almost routine. She dealt with them quietly, hardly breaking the rhythm of her knitting, and it seemed all right to leave her with the station cook while we went off to the party on the wood ship.

It began quietly enough with the ship's officers, the nurses and myself sitting around the captain's cabin sipping gin and tonics. This state of affairs lasted for about three hours until the beefy second officer, who had gone to the station to ask the cook how the woman in labour was getting on, returned, ashen-faced and staggering, to say he had just delivered the baby and would the nurse go over because the cook said that the afterbirth or something wasn't coming as it should and Christ he needed a drink.

As well as the impending New Year we now had something tangible to celebrate, and we moved on to rum to do the event justice. Shoelaces and ties were loosened, and the captain showed us how he could drink a glass of rum standing on his head. He was not a young man and had to be resuscitated after this demonstration, and while I was preoccupied with maintaining an airway, we heard the sound of random small-arms fire from outside.

In fact, this came from some men in the community using ammunition to welcome the New Year, but the captain, lacking oxygen, was lost somewhere among his war experiences.

"Goo' God, they're on us," said the captain, propping himself on an elbow, like the dying Nelson. "Get rid of them, lads, and – good luck." He fell back onto a pillow the second engineer had put under his head. "What a sod," he said.

The others had already clambered up onto the bridge, and by the time I joined them they were setting up a smokescreen to confuse raiders. The smoke came from orange International Distress Flares pouring from five or six cans thrown overboard, which, as it bellowed out over the ice, looked unearthly in the moonlight, the only colour in the white, frozen bay. Someone else was letting off some red parachute flares that looked very pretty, floating into the orange smoke. When they were nearly used up we found some blue pilot flares and some white ones that were so bright they blinded us, turning night into unnatural day. Then the white flare must have melted through the ice and continued to burn underwater, for the surface of the bay suddenly began to shimmer a cold, luminous white. Affected by the huge, peculiar picture that we had created, we all spontaneously joined hands and sang *Auld Lang Syne* with a great deal of emotion, followed by *God Save the Queen* and *Rule Britannia*, with even more emotion.

I walked back to the nursing station as if I had had a psychedelic experience. To add to this sensation, the last thing I saw before I went to bed was the sight of the very fat lady, propped up on pillows and breathing easily, looking down into the crib containing the newborn baby: two very different human beings.

SPRINGTIME: CLINIC IN CONCHE

Spring on the Labrador and in Northern Newfoundland is something that happens at sea while the land is still in the weakening grip of winter. The Arctic sends its flotillas of pack ice southward on the Labrador Current, and with them the seal herds and the fog. The land apparently continues to slumber under its quilt of snow, but there are signs of stirring, flickerings of life in the budding of the birches and movement in the opening brooks, but mostly the winter continues like a depressive old man in a follow-up clinic; maybe some change for the better, but truthfully, none objective. The below-zero days are gone but their replacement by the zephyrs of the summer yet depends on a long haggle with the north. Where the snow has blown away, the milder days are mild enough to soften the earth into mud. Then the ice breaks up, first on the sea, the bays, and the harbours, then on the ponds, and travel is disrupted. Where there are no roads this is felt more keenly. With neither land nor sea accessible, people are temporarily marooned in the settlements and walk between the houses to the still useless stages on gangplanks laid on the mud. This period is called the spring of the year, and the obverse to its damp, miserable side is that of liberation from the winter, that had itself freed us from the autumn but ended as a tyranny.

April 1

I arrived in Conche yesterday and, with the thaw as it is, think this might be the last skidoo trip down the French Shore for this year.

Conche has a road, although the community existed for three centuries before the road was built. People whose livelihood, communications, horizons, customs, folklore, and language were derived from the sea now look to the outside world along a road across the land. Wherever I go I hear stories of men who have sold their nets to buy a car. When the car breaks down – Conche's road sees to that – there is no cash left for spare parts, and no nets left to make cash.

Sailor Jack's is the name of the last hill on the road before Conche. It doesn't take the same way as the old dog team trail, which is vertical, but it is the next best thing. An old man in the clinic, who came down it a thousand times, flattening generations of dogs into the snow with his hurtling komatik, said you don't have God on your side on Sailor Jack's, so he usually got off and walked down.

I was deserted in modern fashion – lost a wheel halfway down and all the oil drained out of the differential casing. It was the front left wheel ("Port for'ard," said the man in the food truck who helped us), and it rolled on ahead in a mocking fashion while we slithered to the edge of a small cliff. It was odd how an accident that nearly finished us off (myself and Helen Sanderson, the nurse at Roddickton) left me cold, and Helen laughing, whereas in England it would have shaken me up. Probably over here the threat of violence is so open and frank that one's original acceptance of it soaks up the reaction to its sudden presence. The wheel was discovered, in the Indian tracking fashion, in the gully, and fixed back on with three bolts, and later with more solid hardware by Ray, the janitor at Conche.

Tomorrow we are going where even four sound wheels can't take us, down the shore to Croque and Grandois: the French Shore.

Conche was tottering between seasons. There was nothing in particular to do except keep the home going, although that was hard enough in itself. But with the bays still frozen there was no fishing, and the next real exertion at the salmon was still far away. Vince Kearney at the store had a small logging operation going down the road, but he hadn't many takers for the work.

"Ain't no hands want to work. They gets their money from the government, the dole."

I met people along the paths between the houses, one man with a team of dogs off to cut firewood.

"Miss Cattell," he said, looking at me, but talking to the nurse, "I got a jaw tooth needs to be hauled." He was a big-boned man, perhaps forty years old, with long arms that his shyness made him use like pendulums weighted with scarred leather mitts. The Blasket Islands off the west of Ireland knew men like this, and being with him I felt as if I was with an endangered species. He had red hair and a complexion of grated carrot to go with it, and an oval, intelligent face, relaxed and smiling. He pointed at me. "I guess he'll make as fine a job as the dentist. My, my, my, that old tooth give me some torment last night." He drew his breath slowly as he remembered the pain.

In the sunshine of Conche we all stood on the sleepy, frozen harbour and thought about his tooth, and then suddenly the communion was broken and we moved off on our separate ways.

I made my way to the community wharf, a well-kept fishing stage of classic design made of white painted spruce. One needed hallucinations and delusions to picture a longliner alongside and the men in rubber clothes, with prongs, unloading a pile of twitching, slimy codfish onto its rough boards. It was standing awkwardly in the frozen sea, welded in the ice and heaped with snow.

Like an Arctic pied piper, I collected a group of children, shedding their shyness as their numbers increased.

"You ain't gonna give us a needle, is you?"

"That's where Mrs. McGrath's old cat sometimes stays." Then pointing to two large holes sawn into a plank overhanging where the water will be, "That's the shithouse." He pointed at a dog on a short chain in a makeshift kennel. "That's a saucy old dog. I's gonna shoot he. Bang." Laughter all around.

They looked healthy, ruddy-cheeked faces topped by sprouting do-it-yourself haircuts. They had wide smiles, even if they were filled with rotten teeth. They wore a mixture of homespun garments, handed down, patched and darned and darned, and much smarter store and catalogue clothes. In many ways they were smaller versions of their parents, their apprenticeships already advanced. There was no separation of the nursery from their pragmatic side of life. It was a continuum. Their games were fishing and the rearing of dolls that looked like knots of rags. They knew how a house was heated because they fetched the wood. They knew where the water came from because they helped carry the pails. The mysteries of the sea had explanations in toil and sweat. And possibly because there was no firm demarcation between childhood and adulthood, the child and the adult lived on in each person at all times of life. That was one of the reasons I liked them so much.

We left early the next morning with two skidoos: Jo Cattell, the nurse, with Ray on the brand new station machine, and I with a man whose name escaped me in the gale of wind that rushed from the gap left behind by nine or ten of his missing front teeth. I later learned his name was Edgar. Our skidoo needed a lot of leaning, because the ridges on the runners that dig into the snow had rusted off. Much of the rest of the skidoo was in the same condition, and it took a lot of starting, pulling the cord over and over while Jo and Ray bounced off down the path ahead of us to the Father McCormack Memorial Airstrip. At last the little uncovered engine, about the same size and appearance as a table-model mincing machine, started up on a final desperate heave that connected his elbow sharply with my nose at the same time, and we chased off, leaning to the left and right and leaving a trail of my blood in case anyone wanted to come after us.

We caught up with Jo, skirted beside the strip, and went down the ice of the back harbour, sloshing through the crusted slob of the ballycatters. There was open water to our right, glinting and ruffled like the gunmetal feathers on a drake's neck, and it made our strip of ice increasingly narrow. At the most precarious point, where the ice was barely fifty yards wide, we were on a slushy path, lined and tracked like a railway junction by previous traffic, with deep cold water on one side and a sheer rocky shore on the other. With the early morning sun on all of this, making the scene a little too sharp to be real, we stopped to discuss whether the ice was strong enough to hold us up. Apparently there was an underwater stream that might have opened earlier that year and hollowed out the ice from below.

I learned from Edgar we were over the worst of it and might as well push on. It was the making of the acceptance of danger.

Once we were off the ice, the energies expended on fear had to be diverted into leg and back muscles, in the act of leaning. I tried to avoid going off the trail, because that is when the skidoo would stop, and in starting it I was not always quick enough to avoid Edgar's elbow; even in the frosty morning, which did away with some of the sensation, I felt that my nose was getting pulpy and was, in fact, intruding into my field of view. Beyond the ice trail were switchbacks, zigzagging, paralleling the coast and making use of ponds. In the short drive we saw evidence of a lot of animal life: spruce partridge, rabbit, otter, beaver, and, near Croque, a big dog fox with a smokestack of a tail ran across our path.

Croque did not have a road and remained traditional, insulated and isolated by the sea, preserving elements of a West Irish culture that most people would think had gone forever. The Irish had followed the French, the Roman Catholic religion staying put. Some of the older people could remember the last of the French, and the community preserved stories of the uneasy handover, tales of fights and hints of murder. Just away from the settlement were wooden crosses marking the graves of French naval seamen of another century. They were poking out of the snow, cleanly painted, maintained to this day by regular visits from French naval ships.

There was very little illness in Croque that concerned me,

and most of what there was could be attributed to the staleness of the season. I was parked with Uncle Ambrose while Jo Cattell went around to the houses doing the real work.

Uncle Ambrose and his wife had prestige as the oldest living inhabitants, but they were respected more for the brightness of their minds than their combined ages of about a hundred and sixty. Their house was small, so small that six people had crowded in with me so there were two to a chair, and no more room round the wall. Without needing much persuasion, Uncle Ambrose started to sing the old-time songs, or the "songs of Grandfather's time." Uncle Ambrose was a portly man and he sat still and sang like a plump choirboy with an old man's tenor, songs of shipwrecks and false-hearted lovers, of sailing ships in foreign lands, of nagging wives and seductive mermaids. In that little room I was transported to another century, in the company of men of that far-off time. In that room, in its size and the way it was built, like the cabin of a wooden ship, and even without the contents of the bottle that was passed round, it was easy to imagine being aboard a ship moored in Poole harbour, taking on a general cargo for Irish ports. I had only to stand and look out of the high window to see fully-rigged ships, and schooners bound for the developing markets in Newfoundland.

I had a small tape recorder with me, but the act of switching it on would have made me into an observer, an eavesdropper from modern times, and outside the dream, so I left it in my bag. Consequently, as with most dreams, I do not remember all the details, certainly not the words of the songs, and, as Uncle Ambrose has since died, the words have gone to his grave with him. Out of all the songs, only one line has stuck in my head, and to say it aloud to myself conjures up that evening like rubbing a genie's lamp. He was singing of his strange lover in one of the songs, and how "her nose was so long that she had to take snuff on a prong."

After the French Shore I drove back to St. Anthony slowly, although Ray said the bolts he had put in should hold until I could send away for the right ones for the Land Rover. The road was well-graded, but even so the drive took seven hours, and the hemispherical sky over the featureless west coast made for soporific monotony. With my eyelids as leaden as the low cloud ceiling, I almost ran over two men who materialized suddenly from the blinkering snow wall on the left side of the road just after Green Island Brook. It felt like a hijack. One of the men was a giant, over six and a half feet, and with wide-set eyes that drilled earnestly into me and out the other side as if he were looking at the horizon beyond. He was dressed in grey, felt-like trousers tucked into knee-length boots and wore a woollen waistcoat over a tartan shirt. In spite of the severe cold, his shirt was open at the neck and his sleeves were rolled up. A knife in a long, partly unstitched sheath was held by some lengths of cord around his waist, and there were streaks of blood on his hands, arms, and face, and matted on his clothes. The other man was smaller, although I did not think I would be able to deal with him any better. He had a knitted hat pulled down to his eyelashes and the rest of his face hidden by a scarf. He was carrying a rifle in a case made out of an inside-out otter skin, and again his hands and clothes were daubed with blood.

"This old jalopy's good for haulin'," said the big one to the other one, eyeing the winch on the front of the Land Rover. And to me: "We fellas got all fooled up in the ice killin' seals and got carried up the shore in the tide. We got a skiff there nipped in the pans."

The road was very near the sea at that point, and by joining all the lengths of rope we had between us we used the capstan winch to pull the heavy boat and its grisly cargo of piled gore from its nest in the rafter ice over the rocks of the foreshore.

I think I have repressed the memory of the lift to Cape Norman I gave to the two men. The smell of blood, rotting fat, old contents of stomachs, rancid seal milk laced with amniotic fluid, and stale urine was just beyond the indescribable. I forget what we talked about.

With the promise of bad weather and the plane just due to cross the Strait of Belle Isle, I felt I had no option but to join it and cross over to Forteau, my next stop, while it was still possible. To anaesthetize myself against the lingering stench of sealers, I had consumed five medicinal fingers of Old Sam rum, and I put the bottle into my bag with a few clean clothes for what might turn out to be a week snowed in up in Forteau. That place is not known for the ready availability of its liquor. Hopefully, I disguised my breath with a little peppermint.

The Mountie usually ruled when the harbour ice was unfit, after the first person had fallen through it, and that time was nearly on us. You could tell if ice was bad from the air if it looked black as you approached to land, but that sign depended on the snow blowing off in patches. That evening we took off from the harbour, possibly for the last time for that year, and headed to the west, flying in the narrow wedge of air between the low clouds and the road I had driven on a half-hour before.

The sea of the Straits was crazy-paved with ice pans, and the red staining on some of them was no reflection from the occasionally glinting low sun, but the transitory evidence of the little tragedies the sealers from Cape Norman had waged in the past few days. Theirs was a hard world, and I thought good luck to the inshore sealers. They risked their lives down there on the heaving ice for a few dollars in conditions no good union man would tolerate for one moment. Except for the money, most of them would admit that sealing had its senseless side, but I felt that without rewards, seals would still be hunted because, in a mountaineer's words, "they were there" and it was one of the rituals of the year.

In Forteau, before I could get into bed, which by then was

all I had in mind, I put a plaster cast on the leg of an old lady who had come to have her "blood took" (blood pressure taken) and slipped on the ice, breaking her ankle.

I slid easily into sleep, although the station was noisy and filled to bursting point with in-patients, and I woke to the dawn chorus of beds being moved and children bawling. My room was that of the "night aide," the local girl who had stayed up all night to keep an eye on the little hospital, and, as her work was over, she was in the room next door with the other girls, waiting for me to get out of her bed.

I lay idly eavesdropping on their chatter, which happened to be about me, and when my conscience licked up from its fire blanket of sleep, I tried not to listen and concentrated instead on the good collection of mottos around the walls. All the girls were of the Brethren sect.

"Dr. Frankel – he ain't saved, is he?"

"No, maid, guess he ain't. Did you smell his breath? Rum. Someone have to work on he."

"Married, too. He's a fast worker."

The motto on the wall straight ahead read, "Only one life, 'twill soon be past, only what's done for Christ will last." Next to it was an exhorting quote from Corinthians in plaster of Paris relief painted with gloomy maroon and dark green. And so on, around the room. It was like the operation room for a holy war.

As breakup progressed, the boats could take to the water and navigate in the moving leads of water, wary of ice and confused by fog.

May 26, Roddickton

I arranged with Chesley Cassell that he will take me to Harbour Deep tomorrow in the *Marlena May*. Tom Decker tells me that with this east wind the ice is being pushed onto the shore and we could be a week or more stuck in Harbour Deep. I can think of worse ways to spend a compulsory week, and have my gun in case there's any birding going on, and a copy of *Tristam Shandy* – and some of the rum is still left. Chesley's telephone is new, and he has an odd way of using it, like many others, shouting abruptly at me as if the amplifier is bad and the telephone company is charging him per word.

"Who talkin'? Doctor? I'm for takin' you if you wants to come. You be here at six the mornin."

We left on time this morning from Englee in a freshening northeaster that had a "nice piece of ice" in the harbour mouth smashing and grinding against the rocks, awash in blues and greens. Ches's longliner, her holds converted for passengers and for carrying the mail, rolled onto her beam ends at each of the Atlantic rollers that were standing upright against the tide coming out of Canada

Bay. We saw two seals swimming in the water a mile off Hooping Harbour, but it was too rough to kill them. My shot with Ches's rusty .22 went at ninety degrees to my aim. We finally gave up and then found that we were in fog.

"No problem to that," said Ches. "That's the b'y going to save us out of this," and he pointed to his dory compass hidden under the slide of its wooden box. "Yes, Doctor, wonderful invention, that compass."

He opened the top and I was dismayed to find the compass card vertical and all the alcohol drained out. I think I would have been dangerously lost. There was an unusual combination of wind and fog, and after a little more than an hour the seas became smaller. We were in the immediate lee of the ice pack. Ches became very serious, although he never lost his good humour. He was continually leaving the wheelhouse to feel the wind, sniff at it, and peer at the seas through the mist. He steered using the same subliminal pointers as migrating birds, synthesizing his course from all the apparent hostility around us. For two hours we went by his knowledge of what the wind did to the tide, and what the tide did to the currents, and how the currents were deflected by the coast. The wind pattern on the waves altered as it veered, and the ice began to come from a new direction. We reached Harbour Deep just in time to dart through a gap of water between the land and the pushing ice pack.

SPRINGTIME: CLINIC IN
FORTEAU, SOUTHERN LABRADOR

The patients had arrived while we ate breakfast, their heads bobbing by the window against the backcloth of pack ice in the Strait of Belle Isle and a mad sky representing every possible type of cloud formation. I held the nine o'clock scheduled radio contact with the hospital at St. Anthony and was told a storm was on the way, then went down to the clinic.

Although there was a door separating the clinic from the waiting room, the gap of about two inches underneath it did away with much of the privacy that it might otherwise have afforded. Not that most people seemed to take privacy very seriously, for I could hear my diagnoses and opinions being discussed freely in the waiting room; and it was, in fact, the chatter which provided the soundproofing. When I had to listen to a heart, or use a stethoscope anywhere else, the nurse would put her head round the door and say hush, and when there was something very secret to discuss we put a transistor wireless in the waiting room as a counterirritant.

I sat at a desk and the nurse called the patients in in the order that they had arrived, giving me their notes, which in many cases went back to the day they were born:

A boy of eleven had warts on his hand that bled when he used an axe or hauled on anything hard enough. He had to chop all the wood for the stove because his father was away in Goose Bay, working in the lumber woods for some extra winter cash. We applied silver nitrate to the lesions on the palm and anterior surfaces of the fingers; it appeared to help sometimes. I asked him if he had been to see old Aunt D., who had no mean reputation for charming warts, and he said that he had, and "it done some good for a spell, sir, but dey come on back."

A regular. A stout, stumpy woman of sixty-five, a broad smile showing pearly false teeth, and wearing a knitted tea-cozy hat with curly grey hair sticking out all the way around. She had "high blood, Doctor" – laughter – "sugar diabetes" – laughter – "wonderful bad nerves" – more laughter. She wanted more nerve pills – Librium, a tranquillizer – because she couldn't sleep "thinking on the crew out on the ice after seals." There was no sugar in her urine and her blood pressure wasn't too bad. She listened, laughing, to the usual advice about dieting, even though I tried to frighten her with the spectres of heart trouble and (much, much worse) a stroke, with all the problems of being bedridden in a house with sparse facilities.

A woman of twenty-seven who was just over six months pregnant and "too big for her dates." She was the daughter of the previous woman and would look just like her one day. Already she had lost her teeth, and her dentures resembled her mother's, tooth for tooth. The nurse, a many times more experienced midwife than myself, thought she had been able to palpate two heads, and did not want to be caught with twins at one of the worst times of the year for transport. There was a family history of twins on her husband's side. I was able to confirm the second head, and felt two backs and more limbs than usual. With the waiting room hushed, almost holding its breath to help me, I heard two fetal hearts, and with the nurse called St. Anthony on the radio telephone to make arrangements for the woman to be taken across the Strait while it was still possible, and to be put in a boarding house until she went into labour.

A powerfully built man, good-looking with fine features, a real Viking. He was fifty years old and had intractable angina pectoris. His father had died at aged forty-nine of a heart attack, so he had it in his mind that he was living on borrowed time, which probably accounted for the melancholy moods that had recently overcome him. He had not been able to walk farther than fifty yards and had to take two or three spells of rest between his door and the government wharf before the chest pains would wear off. With a little trepidation I had started him on propranolol on a previous visit and was pleased to find that he had been helped by it considerably. He was now able to help on the stages and do odd jobs for his sons in the preparation of their fishing gear for the summer.

Another Viking, with all his outdoor clothes on, tweed wool over wool over wool. It was a complicated affair to get to his trouble, which, as he put it, was aft. He had bad piles and got them every year at about that time "through the hauling" (hauling fishing gear). When I was at last able to examine him we found hemorrhoids of the third degree, and I thought he should go to St. Anthony for them to be excised before the summer fishing.

A boy of seven, pulled in unwillingly sideways by his mother. He had a sore throat and it was his third since Christmas. It "punished him to glutch" (swallow), said his mother. "Did he snore?" I asked. She looked at him for an answer. I asked him who he slept with.

"Norm an' Eli an' Eldred, them's me brothers."

"Did they say you snored?"

"Yes, they did."

His tonsils were ragged and unhealthy-looking, inflamed

and covered with debris. His breath smelled bad and he couldn't breathe well through his nose. He took my watch up the stairs to the kitchen away from the din of the waiting room (now discussing piles) and came back saying he could hear the ticking well. We put him on the waiting list for removal of tonsils and adenoids in St. Anthony.

A girl little older than twenty who was nursing a woman at home, bedridden, incontinent, and senile. "And she's nothing to me, only she took my man and reared un when his natural mother died." The old woman shouted at the children and had to be cleaned all the time. The girl wanted to know if they should take the old lady to St. Anthony, but I had to tell her no. As yet there was no provision for that type of care on the coast, and she would have to keep her as long as she lived.

A girl of eighteen, with her teeth miraculously intact and healthy, who came every six months to the doctor to have a heart murmur checked. She had had rheumatic fever at the age of fourteen which had affected her mitral valve, and had been on monthly penicillin injections ever since. She told me she was getting married soon, and the nurse told me she was pregnant and that she would supervise the pregnancy carefully. The girl would have to go to St. Anthony anyway as it was her first baby.

A ruddy-faced man of fifty or so with a rolling fisherman's gait and a mild, bashful manner. His ruddy complexion stopped at a horizontal line halfway up his forehead, where his old tweed cap had sat for much of his life. He showed me his hands which were cracked, raw, and oozing serum, and let me do the talking, coaxing his story out of him with direct questions, and he answering with gentle yeses or nos, speaking in a very characteristic Newfoundland way, on an in-breath. It was the "cold pickle" (seawater) that made his hands like that, and he reckoned he was unable to fish. Unusually for the coast, he was an unmarried man, and fished with his brothers, but this year he had made up his mind to try the welfare. He had an infected allergic-type reaction on his hands, and we treated him with a steroid and antibiotic cream and asked him to come to the nursing station for daily dressings. I filled in a welfare form.

The brother of the previous man, mentally defective, with a screwed-up, asymmetrical face constantly on the move, given to jaw-champing. He was over six feet tall and strong as an ox, and fished with his brothers, although they didn't let him out on the ice. He rarely took his boots off, and now he had an infected toenail. I removed the nail under local anaesthetic and did a wedge resection of the nail bed because the nail had been markedly ingrowing. His feet were very clean.

A powerful woman of forty-seven, her strongly built body draped in a shapeless cotton dress. She was the one whose cheerful, strident voice had been keeping the waiting room gossip and comment going until then. She complained of "wonderful bad hot flashes" and her symptoms had been going on for a year, but lately she had thought she "was losing her mind when the crew was rampsin' round," and she found herself "bawlin' at the maid" (her eldest daughter) who was a good worker, and this upset her mightily. I examined her and did a pelvic examination, including taking a Pap smear, the "cancer test." Except that she was possibly anemic I found nothing and started her on daily hormonal therapy with estrogen. Her hemoglobin was eighty-five per cent of normal, which was about average for a woman of her age in that part of the world.

A mother, pale and pinched, with her youngest son, a wide-eyed, passive sprig of a child, who had a "rising knob in the side of his neck, though I haven't heard him talk of it, and he says he don't find it at all, and he ain't always quiet like that." The child had swollen lymph glands on both sides of his neck and nowhere else. I made a slide for a blood smear and took blood from a vein for other blood tests, but the child, then pounding his mother with rage at the pain I had inflicted on him, looked the picture of health and I doubted that the swollen glands meant anything sinister.

The mother of the little boy with a blistered burn on her skinny right forearm. This burn, or the scar from one, was the hallmark of the women from the outport communities. They got them while baking their bread, putting the loaves in, or removing them from the deep ovens of the stoves.

Another plump "aunt." She wanted her "blood took" and, like an old hand, stripped off her coat, hand-knitted woolly hat, and spectacles, then rolled up her sleeve above her podgy elbows and offered her arm for the blood pressure cuff, all unbidden and methodical. She had been a Methodist, but since the Brethren sect had come to Forteau she had become converted to the new religious denomination.

A man of thirty with a cough that "some says could be the Harn Karn (Hong Kong) flu." He had yellow phlegm and his chest was wild with the noises of bronchitis. His notes in the nursing station were filled with the history of previous chest infections, including the summaries of two admissions to St. Anthony with pneumonia, and we gave him a course of tetracycline. He was leaving the next day to work in Goose Bay in the lumber woods.

A girl of seven, all Irish, with a shock of blonde cumulus hair, darting green eyes, and a self-poised air, poking her nose. She had come out in a rash, said her mother, "and we says it's the itch." The rash was all over her body, and she was undressed down to her knickers, and when these were dropped she rebuked her mother in a whisper. "You said he wouldn't take 'em ALL off." Her mother was right with her diagnosis. The rash was that of scabies, and we gave her benzyl benzoate for all her eight children.

A woman who could have been any age, with a big, round face and features blunt to the exclusion of all teeth. Her body had the form of the sacks of flour and potatoes that were nine tenths of her diet, and she complained of backache, front ache, side ache, and pains anywhere I cared to mention. Her husband had died "last fall twelvemonth," possibly from neglect, and now she had let herself go and looked as if she would soon join him. "Shoot me like an old dog, I ain't fit regard o' nuthin'." It was so easy to miss depression, because the symptoms of misery and wretchedness were so often related to the inability to work or to physical symptoms. There was little or no vocabulary for introspection except for generalizations like "low-spirited" or "bad nerves," and the pathways to the psyche were overgrown with somatic brambles that snared the unwary. We admitted this woman to St. Anthony for treatment by the psychiatrist, and under his care she did well.

A man of forty-two, limping in to shake my hand with a firm, thorny grip. I knew that he had crushed his left leg last year when an engine he was lowering into a new boat had come adrift and landed on him. Now he had a big effusion in the knee joint and crepitus on all movements. He had returned from his rabbit snares and reckoned that he was "working against himself," labouring all day in rackets (snowshoes) in the deep, wet snow. "Catch any rabbits?" "Five," he said cheerfully, "but not sure that ain't enough ter fill the insides of a she-capelin. Rabbits makes poor eating." We put an elastic bandage on the knee and told him to rest, although we knew the impossibility of that.

A woman with a letter for me to take to her daughter who was away in St. Anthony waiting for her first baby.

Yet another "aunt," only this one was born in 1885, and in her case she probably was everyone's aunt. She had a healing burn on her forearm to testify she still made her own bread, and she sported a very ripe black eye, caused when she fell off her grandson's skidoo going to a wedding a few days back. She was anxious that she would be disfigured for life and seemed doubtful when I reassured her, going over to look at herself in the mirror. She told me she had shaken Dr. Grenfell's hand and that he had saved her first-born who had fallen in the brook and caught "the pneumonia."

The daughter of the previous woman came to have me check her hypertension, which in recent months had been high enough to give alarming symptoms. She had been having morning headaches, "picks of light dancing in her eyes," and had been getting short-winded at night. Her blood pressure was 220/130 millimetres of mercury despite treatment with reserpine and a diuretic, and since the last time I had examined the fundi of her eyes, she had developed a retinopathy with exudates and one small flame hemorrhage. She had always had "high blood" ever since her pregnancies (of which she had been through eleven, but buried nine "with the TB"). On examination, the apex beat of the heart was displaced further than the last time, and the second heart sound was accentuated. She had crepitations (rattling sounds) at both lung bases. An electrocardiogram showed evidence of myocardial enlargement and ischemia (lessened blood flow to the heart), and the tracing was altered from the one we had taken two months previously. She agreed to come into the nursing station for the rest and for starting on new treatment. She was adamant that she did not want to go to St. Anthony because travel at that time of year was precarious, and it may have been several weeks before she would be able to get back to L'Anse au Loup where she lived.

One of the rare girls requesting birth control advice. She already had two kids after being married for eighteen months, "and didn't want ne'er another for yet a while." She had made up her mind to be fitted with "the machine you puts inside" – an intrauterine device – and after making sure she was suitable for one, I did put one inside. She was one of the more modern girls, who had lived for a few years in Goose Bay, and was now dressed more fashionably than most, in a trouser suit from the catalogue and her hair in curlers under a scarf.

A man of thirty-eight, black curly hair, and an olive complexion with fine features, who, in his blue fisherman's jersey, was the spitting image of his Basque ancestor. He had a complicated story of pains in his side, which was always an ill-defined area, and his description inconsistently traced and rerouted the symptom into his arms, back and down his right leg. He wanted to be "all cured up for the salmon" but did not seem to be all that keen to get better. When symptoms were not based on my ideas of anatomy and physiology, I turned over a few stones looking for neurotic creepy-crawlies, or worse. With the transistor wireless playing in the waiting room, and the nurse tactfully absented, he told the story of a disturbed, depressed man, "still owin' for last summer's rig-out an' no ways to make a nickel," gloomily accepting the possibility of suicide. I tried to trace out his relation with his family, probing his feelings and emotions with an instrument that must have to be all the sharper because of his inability to respond. His children were "all right, I suppose," and his wife was a "good worker." He said he had "lost me nature" – become impotent – and that he had been "with a no-good kind of woman down Goose Bay" and the way he said it was full of his guilt. He would not go to St. Anthony, and I thought it was worthwhile to prescribe an anti-depressive drug. In a very short twenty minutes I hoped I had given him something to think about, new ways to consider himself.

A cough in a big-bosomed Viking's wife, and she gave me a hearty demonstration. A real fishwife that one, a repository of knowledge on everything in the Newfoundland book. The cough was dry and unproductive and we gave her a bottle of codeine linctus to suppress it, but it was only as she left that I realized that she was not satisfied. She had made up her mind it was either tuberculosis or the "canister" (cancer) and thought she should go to St. Anthony for a chest X-ray. She gave the bottle of linctus back to me with a reproachful look in her eyes.

The last patient. A young-looking man of thirty-five with very fair hair and one of those pink glowing complexions like good quality porcelain. Unbelievably, he had been waiting his turn for an hour, with a big longlining hook embedded in the web at the base of his thumb. The technique of removing a hook is to saw through its distal part and then work it through the flesh in the direction it was designed to go. The barb would cause too much damage if it were pulled backward.

A TRIP TO THE ICE

I had been waiting for some bushings for an abused shock absorber in my Land Rover and had drifted over to the St. Anthony radio telephone office to see if they had arrived. On my way over, trudging through the slushy snow, I met the pilot of the helicopter which is rented by the hospital at breakup time, when the melting ice makes orthodox bush flying impossible. The helicopter had also been out of order, and the pilot, too, was looking for a spare part. He was a Texan, lately employed on a gunship in Vietnam, and in his deadpan drawl he told me that he was speaking to the pilot of the mail plane, who yesterday saw the first sign of the seal herds, about ten miles offshore from Belle Isle. Enforced idleness had kept the two of us together in the past few days, but now I said no to our chess and crate of beer routine and told him I must be on my way again.

I hoped the bushings would be three more days late.

Since March I had had a standing invitation to go sealing with a man from near Cape Onion. My friend at Cape Onion had no electricity, or much else in the way of "mod cons" at his house, and I telephoned another man who might have known of his plans. Everyone seemed to know the seals were there; the people of the north coast had pointed the herd like hunting dogs, and I sensed the eagerness as I spoke on the phone. The man I talked to said that three of them were going the next day at dawn. "Bless you, my dear," he said. "There's thousands of room for another hand."

The names of the men are secret. They used illegal methods to kill the seals. I'll call them Ham, Shem, and Japheth, which is close to the spirit of their real names anyway.

I had been out on the pack ice before. Unlike most hazards, it seemed worse the closer one came to it. From afar it was placid, like acres of featureless plain, as motionless as islands unless one had patience to gaze for an hour or more. In that time the pack pushed along about a mile on the current, more if the breeze was with it. Close to, as seen from a boat coming alongside to "land" someone, it was horrifying. The sea, suddenly brought to life, swirled and swilled between the weirdly sculpted blocks, sucking at the man on them as if he were a strand of meat caught between rotten teeth. The blocks were large, each as big as a house, and what looked white from afar turned out at close quarters to be eerier turquoise, or dark, opaque greens where the Atlantic seas pushed over the jostling ice, breaking and foaming as over a shoal, and cool swimming pool colours away from the edge. Its apparent static quality

– which was accentuated as one approached in a small boat because the pack acts as a breakwater to dampen the ocean swell – was really a constant plunging, swaying, and tilting that seemed to contain deliberate malice. The pack ground, together with creaks and bellows from air trapped in caverns underfoot, sent up exploding plumes of Atlantic water. On an overcast day, muting the scene with a wash of grey with evening drawing on, an ice pack must be the most godforsaken place on land or water on which a man could find himself. But as we chugged up through the Strait of Belle Isle, the dawn, at least, had the promise of light and, as I saw it then, the not unpleasant threat of the day.

Shem sat in the bow, his parka hood up against the east wind, whittling the final touches to the butt of a .22 pistol that he had converted from an old rifle by sawing down its barrel and removing the original butt. He loaded it and stuck it in his belt, the barrel pointing to his groin. It was illegal to have a pistol, but Shem took less chance with the Mountie than with blasting his genitalia to kingdom come. Ham steered with his ungloved hand on the outboard motor, coaxing it between choke and throttle as it spluttered. He was my host, and huddled in the stern beside him I talked to him of seals, and of what I should do on the ice. Japheth was a mystery man who kept much to himself, jerking glances at me, but mostly lost in what I took to be thoughts. His face had a periodic tic in the muscles around the eyes that led on to a paroxysm of shoulder movements and head-shaking, mirthless laughter. He was very strongly built, slung on the thwart like a great ape, with very little neck and massive hands, the palms turned out, swinging on long arms. His thumbs were very short – one of my own unexplainable pointers to an abnormal mind.

As we neared the pack, threading through the outpost "growlers," it seemed impossible that there could be any life on it; its very nature of orderless hostility was the antithesis of living things, least of all the big, furry, lovable mammals and their podgy white infants that we were after for the killing.

The motor gave up on its own accord, and we sculled to the nearest landing point, the punt nicely wedged between two rocking, underwater platforms, and we clambered onto the ice. The men carried long gaffs, used for killing the seals, for vaulting from one piece of ice to another over a gap of sea, and for hauling two blocks together with a man pulling on each end. Shem had his pistol out and Japheth a bolt-action rifle with the safety catch off and a round in the breech. No one spoke, not even a curse for a boot full of turquoise water when the precarious edge gave way. We were "in the fat" all right; there were seals all around us, unaware and placid, blobs of bodies reaching away in the distance like basking tadpoles. One near us looked around at its infant, a white oval burrowing for the tit, and I could see the whites of her eyes, chalky white and shot with blood against the sparkle of the ice. The mother belched and the breeze brought a warm, sour smell of rotting fish over to us.

Japheth lifted his rifle, holding the weapon casually away from his shoulder, and shot the mother. Ham and Shem jumped up, sprinting like soldiers out of the trenches, plunged their sharp gaffs into the faces of two bewildered harp seals, and then kicked the disabled animals on their soft snouts. Shem shot another, a bedlamer, with his pistol before it could reach the water, and Japheth picked up the whitecoat (the baby seal) and threw it down as a fish might be killed – indeed, some regard them as fish. Shem took hold of Japheth's rifle and shot another in the water, but it sank before anyone could get a gaff on it.

The killing was over as suddenly as it began. They were pleased with the four seals and ignored the others: too late to catch them – they were sliding, rolling, bellyflopping into the pools all round us, yodelling and splashing, scores of them. In ten seconds the ice pack was as deserted as the other side of the moon. Sharp knives were produced and we vaulted over to the pan of ice, where Shem had shot the seal with his pistol, and pulled the corpse back from the edge. He was delighted with his aim. The bullet had entered the ear and come out of the eye at the other side of the head, the classical way to leave a pelt unharmed. He skinned it, peeling off the pelt and its three-inch lining of yellow fat. Ham was working on another and showed me the pelt. As I did what he told me, hot blood gushed out of the seal and melted a shallow, smooth trough in the swaying ice, covering my boots in gore and leaving us standing in the steam of a musky, post-mortem smell. On the next pan, Japheth had found a heart that was still beating in his seal, and on a ghoulish impulse he cut it out and tossed it to me, the tic in his face wild and now mixed with a smile. It was the closest we ever came to a relationship. I caught the heart and watched it die, allowing myself mixed feelings as the follow-up to the carnage continued. The heart looked very human, as did the appealing eyes of the mother seal shot first. Another baby whitecoat was found, this one unborn, but delivered by caesarean section as its mother was skinned.

We had four good pelts and two whitecoats, a cargo worth about eight dollars, and we dragged them all back to the boat and persuaded the outboard motor to start. The dawn was over, its blood-red sky concentrated into our load of clotted gore. As we went in the smooth water near Great Sacred Island, my appetite for breakfast displaced all my disapproval for what the Cape Onion sealers had done, and any possible conscience I might have had for being involved as an accessory after the fact of their morning's work.

I have written of the illegality of our operation, and we were certainly out on the ice under assumed names. Several laws were broken, and cheerfully so, because, as I was told, they lacked good sense and logic. It had been ruled far away from the realities of pack ice, that a baseball bat, or a weapon very much like one, was the fairest instrument for battering a seal to death. The use of the gaff had been made unlawful. The ethics of good sportsmanship were forcefully introduced into an arena where they had no natural place. Explain it to a Cape Onion sealer, a kind, sensible man like Shem, for example, that he has to clamber over the grinding pack ice without the help of the pole of his gaff, nor anything to offer another man who has slipped down and needs a handhold. Tell him that he has to take on an enraged hood seal, she with the frenzy of a mother protecting her young and he armed with a baseball bat. He will quietly tell you where to stuff your laws.

The other laws we broke were the carrying of the pistol, the shooting of the seal in the water, and the killing of the whitecoat. The young seals, with their soft, snowy fur, make valuable objects in the shops in Montreal and Toronto when stuffed, and the skins fetch a good price from the taxidermist. If the sealers themselves saw any injustice, it was that the price given for the carcasses were so low – two and a half dollars in 1970 – that an incredible amount of meat had to be left behind on the ice, an appalling waste to the thrifty mind.

The seals that we killed were "harp" seals – Phoca groenlandica, as the classifiers have it – and they had in fact come with the ice all the way from Greenland and the Arctic waters of Baffin Bay. The Newfoundlanders have a word for each stage of their development; Ham outlined it for me as we were on our way to the ice.

"There's whitecoats, them's the pups – cats, some calls them – and their mothers, called harps. Now, there's old harps and young harps according to their age, and younger than that they're bedlamers. And after bedlamers they're rusties – for the darkedy patch comes on their backs. That's the patch looks like a harp, some says.

"On times, us catches an old hood – that's another breed. Us be too handy on the shore to see any hoods the morning. Hoods is bigger than harps, and saucy, b'y, I'll guarantee you. Takes two hands to kill an old hood, say, me and buddy there." – He points to Japheth. "I runs behind and kicks she in the scutts, and buddy taps she in the smellers with the gaff, and then shoves her on down. And she roarin', roarin', my dear man, like the devil's own to-do."

I saw some hoods two days later, when again I met the helicopter pilot and he said his spare part had been fitted, and did I want to come to try her out? We flew north to Belle Isle and, then, satisfied the machine was working well, crossed some open water to the ice that supported the seal herd. With his Vietnam training of assessing numbers of individuals from the air, he said we were looking down on two hundred thousand seals. He lowered the helicopter and we hovered over a big hood seal. I understood Ham's respect for the animal; it was indeed roaring like the devil's own to-do, and even from our safe perch I experienced a shiver of fright. It inflated the big hood of skin over its head and gave a prolonged roar that was more defiance than fear, and I could see what I took to be tonsils. Other seals were crashing into the water as they had during my skirmish on the ice two days previously. I was glad I was no longer a hunter.

Top: Dr. Miles Frankel on a skidoo in Labrador, 1971. (Frankel family photo)
Bottom: Dr. Miles Frankel travelling by dog team. (Frances Astor photo.)

Miles on board his yacht, *Conche*, 1971. (Frankel family photo)

Miles taking a reading from the sun with his sextant on board his yacht, *Conche*, 1971. He later developed partial blindness in his right eye from solar maculopathy. (Frankel family photo)

Top: Miles Frankel's yacht, *Conche*, showing the Swiss flag and the Canadian emblem. Bottom: The Frankel yacht, *Conche*, on the North Atlantic seas.

(Frankel family photos)

A typical coastal community served by the International Grenfell Association.
(Frankel family photo)

A remote outport on the west coast of the Great Northern Peninsula.
(Frankel family photo)

Typical outport scenes.
(Top, Candace Cochrane photo; bottom, Frankel family photo)

Old and new technologies. Dog teams and aircraft were essential to provide services by the International Grenfell Association. (Frances Astor photo)

Carrying the mail. (Joan Cattell photo)

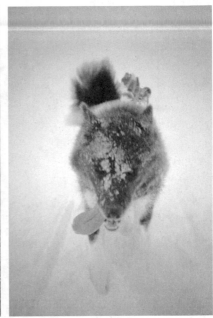

Labrador sled dogs.
(Top left photo, Candace Cochrane; top right and bottom, Frances Astor)

Sled dog teams in Labrador. (Frankel family photos)

Sled dog teams in Labrador. (Frances Astor photos)

Dog team on the path from Roddickton to Conche.
(Joan Cattell photo)

Mug-up along the road. (Joan Cattell photo)

Forestry plane landing in Roddickton, nursing station in background centre. (Candace Cochrane photo)

Dog team outside the Roddickton IGA station. (Joan Cattell photo)

Loading pulp on the ship at Roddickton. (Candace Cochrane photo)

Englee IGA nursing station. (Candace Cochrane photo)

Mission plane used by the IGA, in Conche harbour. (Joan Cattell photo)

Conche harbour. (Joan Cattell photo)

Unloading a seal in Conche. (Joan Cattell photo)

Conche. (Joan Cattell photo)

Unloading a patient at St. Anthony. (Candace Cochrane photo)

Hospital plane. (Joan Cattell photo)

Top: A fisherman in Newfoundland dealing with his catch.
(Frankel family photo).

Bottom: People and activities in
northern communities.
(Frances Astor photo)

Dog team returning a patient to Conche. (Joan Cattell photo)

An example of the isolation faced by communities without roads.
(Candace Cochrane photo)

Radio telephone operator at St. Anthony, a vital link to nursing stations.
(Candace Cochrane photo)

Steamers in St. Anthony. (Joan Cattell photo)

IGA pilot picking up patients for the St. Anthony hospital.
(Candace Cochrane photo)

Roddickton. Loading a patient on the hospital plane headed for St. Anthony.
(Candace Cochrane photo)

Nurse helping a patient at the Roddickton nursing station.
(Candace Cochrane photo)

Nurse Cattell operating on a sled dog puppy. (Joan Cattell photo)

Top: Photo of an iceberg taken from Miles's yacht, *Conche*, off the coast of Newfoundland, 1971. (Frankel family photo)

Bottom: The greatest navigation threat down North – ice. (Candace Cochrane photo)

Strathcona docked at a wharf in Nain. (Candance Cochrane photo)

Inuit family heading for the *Strathcona* north of Nain.
(Candace Cochrane photo)

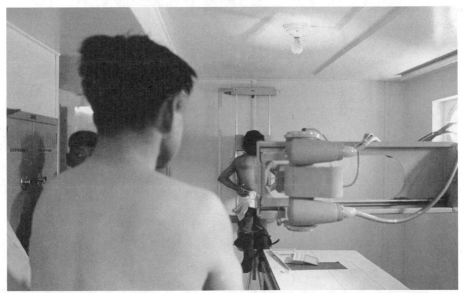

Getting TB X-rays aboard the *Strathcona*. This was a standard activity once the
Christmas Seal no longer made the rounds. (Candace Cochrane photo)

Williamsport whaling station from the air, 1970. (Candace Cochrane photo)

Williamsport whaling station. (Candace Cochrane photo)

FISHING

It is difficult to name the natural first day of a season: the seasons merge, one with the next. But I suppose summer in Newfoundland begins on the day when the capelin first come in. The Newfoundlanders call this sign the "capelin scull." The arrival of the capelin is eagerly awaited because it heralds the appearance of codfish, who devour the capelin in great numbers; and the Newfoundlanders have a similar interest in the cod. Until the fisherman catches a fish with a capelin in its stomach, the year has not truly begun.

But although the finding of a capelin inside a codfish is an auspicious sign, it lacks the drama of the capelin scull. Millions upon millions of sprat-like silvery fish come to the beaches, to the very edge of the sea, to spawn. The wavelets in the sheltered bays land them on the sand and the rocks and strand them, and they die in vast numbers. They can be scooped up live from the shallow water by the bucketful, and taken home and fried, or piled on the bad soil to make it fertile for growing potatoes. They are transitory and have no commercial value. This has changed, but to the fishermen the sign of the capelin is their star in the East, a promise of greater things to come.

It would be a wonderful education for all eaters of frozen fish fingers and pies to spend a summer with a Newfoundland inshore fisherman. If the fish are plentiful, the price is often low, and if they are not the very real toil becomes more than discouraging. I only once saw fishermen make a lot of money, when the price was good and they were getting a lot of fish.

I went with Bob P. hauling his mackerel nets and cod traps. He has two fleets of mackerel nets out, and a trap by the Mad Moll. We left in the dawn with a fine mackerel sky, almost blood red, which augured well for catching mackerel. And catch them we did. There was a ripple on the water as we approached the nets, and even from our low angle in the trap boat I could see that the patch of water around the net buoys was silver with snared fish. The nets catch them by the gills or round the middle if they are not on the small side.

Each mackerel has to be taken out of the net, one at a time, before we could move on to the next net. By "taking" I mean ripping, which often comes to partial decapitation. The fish were nearly all alive, and in filling the boat the summation of pain we caused must have been enormous. Bob was really excited.

"Money over the side, money over the side, me b'ys," he kept shouting, and, "There's a dress for the woman, my oh my, money over the side." It must have been a long time since he filled up a boat with fish like that. It took four hours to fill it.

All hands were summoned to the stage when the catch was brought in, and a good catch was unusual enough to put smiles on everyone's face. Anyone who could walk helped to empty the boat of mackerel, shovelling them into pails and emptying the pails into the barrel by the gutting table. The oldest of Bob's children was twelve, and the youngest was four, and they all did their share without a word from their father. As the boat was unloaded, so Bob and his eldest daughter filleted the fish and put the fillets into a barrel. Six hours had gone since the pre-dawn breakfast and there was still another trip to the nets to be made, more ripping of five thousand mackerel from the sea, and more layering the white parts of their bodies into barrels. The barometer was falling, and tomorrow the weather will make it less pleasant, or even impossible, to take the fish while they were still there.

Besides fishing I lanced water pups (the small boils that appear on the wrists of the fishermen), gave "baby needles" (vaccinated infants), excised a lymphoma, changed a plaster of Paris splint, prescribed and counted out an anti-depressive drug, prescribed and counted out "blood pressure pills," assessed a heart murmur, and referred a child with warts to a wart charmer in a nearby settlement. I had learned from one of the old women how to prepare a bread poultice, and extracted four teeth from three separate heads. I was ready to move on to the next settlement, and now that the boat was unloaded of mackerel I lay in the sun on the stage and watched the deft movements of Bob's daughter as she filleted her catch.

For the half of the year that the sea is in its liquid form, the fishing stages were the centres from which all activity was measured. The daily plunder of the sea was broken only by a strict day of Sunday rest; for the working week, the stage was at the hub of land, air, and sea, the sparse trinity of the Newfoundlander.

In a part of the bay where protection from wind and lop was greatest, tucked in behind the point, or in a tickle in the lee of an island, the stages were made as platforms which level off the sloping rocks of the shore. The land is usually treeless as far as the eye can see, and the spindly construction of the stages, with their tree-trunk supports finding what purchase they could on ledges and crannies in the bedrock, were like substitute trees and I thought of them as part of the Newfoundland vegetation.

Near the stage was built a shed that was a workshop and a storeroom. There was a door to the shed, but no lock – maybe only a wooden latch, pulled up by a loop of twine through a hole in the door.

Inside the stage it was dark, and probably lit only by the chinks of light through the planking walls. The floor was uneven, piled with coiled nets, some still containing the debris of the sea, and in the darkness along the wall were crouched a row of barrels: some open, of light-coloured oak, others with their lids on and full of salted mackerel. There was one big barrel that was dark with age – it was probably older than the stage, or even the settlement. (Maybe it came over on a British man-o'-war after the Treaty of Utrecht.) It was slimy and covered with a creeping excrescence and was filled almost to the brim with cod livers.

Farther down the stage were stacked bags of salt with some cork floats and coils of nylon rope over them. A prong leaned against a wall by a tiny glassless window, and beside it was a wooden barrow, with a wooden wheel, filled with tied longlining hooks. At the far end was a gutting table, much used, gouged, and stained with blood, and a hole in the floor to one side of it for the jettisoning of fish stomachs. The stomachs could be seen in the water below, swaying in the gentle surge like bloodless sea fauna; not more strange than anything else in the mysterious sea.

At the end farthest from the sea was a neat stack of split, dried, and salted codfish, ivory-coloured with dark skins, like a pile of antiquarian books opened at different references. This pile of fish was the summer harvest. It was also the key to the smell of the stage. The twang of fish harmonized with every olfactory note. Above all there was the rank blast suppressing the pleasant smell of tarred twine and the soupy sea smells bubbling out of the tide's ebb, sharp iodine and the softer tones of putrefaction. The discerning could sense pine sap and an undertow of burnt engine oil.

It is a mixture of sights and smells that is the quaintness of Newfoundland. The rickety stages are a blend of spartan and the homely, the impermanence of the nomad, and the conservatism of the Celt. Each stage is a monument to the independence of the man who built it. There is no one to buy a stage from, no stages to buy, no stage-building contractors. Fishing is an expression of a way of life, not an occupation for working hours; and fishing begins and ends at the stages.

Going out fishing was recreation for me, something I could fit in between my clinics, and, even if it was taxing or exhausting or repetitive or occasionally frightening, it put a charge into my batteries and refreshed me. It also made me glad I was not a fisherman, nor had to be. The combination of the unblinking eye of the sea, watchful and unforgiving from one horizon to the other, the solitary work in an open boat that is hard physical effort with cold fish and cold water, the certainty that most days are worked for nothing, and that each man is dependent only on himself to break even, means that a man had to be born to it to take the burden of that way of life. It is the same with coal miners. Who else could take on such hardship, and at the same time consider it modestly and without question, if he had not been isolated from the comfortable world of inheritance?

We had corned fish for supper and a great sodden pile of brewis (pronounced *broos*) to go with it. Corned fish is dried and lightly salted cod that the fisherman makes for his own immediate use: it won't keep for much longer than a week. Brewis is hardtack biscuits soaked overnight in water – a sort of substitute vegetable. (Uncle Charley says he likes his soaked in cold tea.) Over the mound of pale nourishment go "scruncheons," little chips of pork fat pan fried with onion and poured on with the liquid grease. Fish and brewis is the so-called national dish of Newfoundland, and many tourists, eager to taste the country's fare, must have poisoned themselves on it. In fact, it hardly makes sense to eat it unless one has been out for some time in a small boat. Fish and brewis is a fitting and delicious end to a day's fishing.

With the clinics over (and the aircraft held at bay behind low cloud), I went out jigging for cod today. I bought a jigging hook last month in Harbour Deep and have carried it about like a talisman ever since. It is a lead fish, marked like a cod, about eight inches long with twin hooks curling out of its mouth, and a hole in its tail for attaching the line.

I rowed out into the bay with Aeseph – called Ace

– and "lined up" the shore marks to put us over a shoal where he thought the fish would be. We calculated Old Harry's sunkers, by using the church as a marker, and the low end of Dog Island with a white spot halfway up the cliff beyond, in fact a small boat thrown and lodged there in a storm.

Jigging is a simple technique of catching fish. The only difficulty is to keep going for longer than several hours. The lead fish is lowered until it touches the bottom of the sea, then raised about three feet. All there is left to do is to jerk the line up and down until a fish is caught on the hook. If the boat is in the right place this could be on the first upward movement. The fish are seldom caught by the mouth. The hook finds their fin or belly or tail, and it is this that shows how thick they must be on the bottom. It is like firing a gun into a crowd of people; however bad a shot you are, you are bound to hit someone.

One advantage of being out at sea was the avoidance of flies. I never seemed to give them much of an appetite, but the children of the outports, especially the fairer ones, and the nurses from England and America and mainland Canada, with their pink, soft skins, provided easy meat. The flies were the bane of the summer, and even if they did not bite me, they swarmed about my head as a high-pitched nuisance and were sometimes thick enough to obscure the view, curdling the clarity of most fine summer days. They were worst in the forested parts and where the land sheltered the settlement from the prevailing wind. The blackflies could denude the surrounds of the eyes of skin, until the face streamed with blood and all the soft tissues were laid open to infection. It was curious how some people attracted the blackflies, carrying their dark, dancing halo throughout the summer, while others walked free. I had the halo but not the bites. Some days I was free of flies altogether, yet spent half the day treating children who had been bitten worst. The Newfoundlanders needed a patron saint to banish the flies from their country, just as St. Patrick rid Ireland of snakes. Perhaps St. Anthony could be persuaded.

The last noteworthy feature of any introduction to the summers of Newfoundland and Labrador is the procession of the icebergs, flotillas of the Arctic navy on their way to the breaker yards of the south. Until the consideration enters one's head that they had travelled from their calving in Greenland as far as this at the rate of one mile an hour, the presence of such mountains of ice in the summer seems paradoxical. They are alpine in form, texture, and colour, detached marine alps with very little future. Their shapes are sculpted on massive lines, by erosion from their lashing by the seas, which they cause to break, and from a continuous process of melting. Some are faced like the Matterhorn, others are pillared like the ruins of unimaginable temples. On sunny days, waterfalls of fresh Greenland water cascade into the sea and mix their spray in the permanent rainbow from the Atlantic waves exploding under the lower overhangs. Icebergs are said to smell, but much as I ever sniffed at them, I never did catch the scent of one. Before radar, the only chance the mariner had in fog was a snatch of scent from some rotting organic debris caught in the ice.

I, of course, found the icebergs beautiful, and watched them often. I once saw one turn over to reach a new equilibrium. It was in the middle distance, but even from afar, and without the benefit of sound, it was a sight of great natural violence. I was looking at it and realized it must be a big one since it looked large enough though two miles away. Then, suddenly, a lower cornice fell away and the berg lost its balance. Thousands of tons of ice toppled to the left until the nine tenths that everyone knows is underwater swung up to prove its existence. A big roller struck the unstable berg at that moment and lifted one side. As if a battleship had been blown up, the iceberg rolled and smashed against the sea, and then rolled the other way and turned right over.

I was unable to sleep last night in Sandy Hook, notwithstanding that the place has, for me, an atmosphere of built-in peace. Alexis Bay and the sea to the horizon are full of icebergs. We counted one hundred and six from the top of the island. All night, great chunks of ice were falling off them, fracturing with a crack like sharp thunder, and crashing into the sea. It was like being involved in an artillery battle.

The fisherman hates the iceberg. They are a hazard to his boats and his nets, and they run aground and block the entrance to the coves. In the south they have to be towed clear of the oil rigs, and there is a rumour that they take them up to Miami for the rich folks to put bits of glacier ice, thousands of years old, into their cocktails. In the north that sort of behaviour is outlandish. Like much of the Newfoundlanders' world, ice is yet another enemy without malice.

Just as it is difficult to name the first day of summer, the end of the season is even more vague. The fish gradually become scarcer, the cold makes going out in an open boat too much of a burden, the schools in the winter settlements begin, and enough stamps have been earned to pay for the winter's unemployment. The season fizzles out; four short months in which to have made a living for the year. But like everything where life is composed of extremes, the short beauty of the summer has its compensations.

Except for some recalcitrant mineral substances in my teeth, where the metabolic turnover of the body's molecules is slowest, in two years I ate my way into becoming a Newfoundlander. There are theories that one eventually becomes what one eats, and in attempting to give inside information on the Newfoundland people, my interest in promoting these theories is not exactly selfless. Sadly, in the years since leaving Newfoundland, I have eaten myself into being a Frenchman, an Englishman, a Papuan, and an Irishman, and the Newfoundlander that I was is a man of history. I am the weaker for it.

Usually I ate in the nursing stations, or in people's homes in the districts served by the stations. Hunger is the best sauce, so it is said, and I learned gradually to spice my hunger with appetite. I had to learn to enjoy the food, which, when I arrived in the country, I would have classed as subsistence for those stranded in the wilderness, bizarre viands to sustain them as they made their way to the juicy steaks and pommes frites of civilization. Almost all the food was grown, netted, hooked, trapped, hunted, or picked locally. Only a few essentials – flour, yeast, sugar, tea – came in from the outside, and when they failed to come, life was hard to bear.

How many people have eaten thin stews of porcupine and muskrat, braised whale steaks and black seal flipper pie, fat cod tongues and gristly caribou, moose liver and roasted Labrador owls, fish and brewis, polar bear and black bear, salmon, and yet more bloody salmon, and capelin fried as they spawned and committed suicide on the beach? I stuffed myself with bakeapples, partridgeberries, squashberries, blackberries and blueberries, fresh in a hand-to-mouth way, or bottled or made into pies, after I had eaten boiled rabbit or roasted turr or boiled duck; and forbidden, protected Canada goose served with long, dusky-skinned potatoes, and cabbage and turnips. I gorged on spruce partridge and white partridge, or on smelts caught through an ice hole, and once, deliciously, an Arctic char. I drank Newfoundland screech, rough, cheap rum, and made my head go around on illegal and sedimented homebrews, and on amateur but effective distillates so filled with impurities that the mind and the liver boggled in dealing with them. I sipped water on sunny days from pools on ice pans, and put the Arctic ice from giant bergs, thousands of years old, into my whisky glass. I drank strong tea made of peaty, soft, iodine-coloured water with cows' milk, weak from poor grazing, and spread pale butter onto warm, crispy bread.

I forsook my slender possibility of entering heaven by dropping live Port au Choix lobsters into boiling water, and supped on mussels and periwinkles – mushels and wrinkles – from Sandy Cove, and clams from Anchor Point. I ate great halibut steaks and huge plates of herring and mackerel before they lost the colours of the sea.

Mostly, however, I existed on the codfish, which in summer was always there for the taking and could be served in any number of ways, most often being boiled with onions and pork fat and garnished with scruncheons.

Pigs that fend for themselves on the seashore, rooting in the organic flotsam of the sea, are said to develop a fishy taste in their flesh, and if on my travels I had been stranded, with cannibalism the only means to survival, I think my companions would have found me the same way.

And as anyone who likes to eat will tell you, the ambience of the meal is as subtle an enzyme in its digestion as the juices of the stomach. Perhaps one can become an Italian by eating pizzas and pasta in London, or Japanese by guzzling raw fish in expensive and authentic restaurants in Paris, but for the man to become what he eats he should do his eating in the area where the food is produced.

In my case, the Newfoundland carbohydrates, fats, and proteins entered me directly from their natural surroundings. They were spiced by the blessing of the meal and the talk of the table, the children playing about my stockinged feet with a gin trap and a razor-sharp hatchet; and afterward, roasting myself by the stove, accompanying my digestion with the playing of noisy and complicated card games, and joining in talk of politics, fishing, weather, and grievances.

And, as the evening became night, I lay in a deep featherbed in an alcove off the kitchen, listening to an old man feathering splits for the morning fire, breathing a low, monotonous tune with Gaelic modes, an old woman, snoring not far away through a thin wall, her teeth, bought that morning "off-the-peg" from the store along the bay, on a table beside her, a child having a bad dream and a sister awakening to comfort her, a dog starting a scrap outside and another howling lazily at the hazy moon – then the meal becomes the man.

VETERINARY ADVENTURES

Along the northern tip of the island of Newfoundland and its coast at the Strait of Belle Isle, where the long grass could be cut for hay and easily carted, the fishermen kept cows and the farmers went out to fish. Elsewhere, on the Labrador Coast and on the more hilly east side of the island, the hay was harder to come by, and in any case canned milk and margarine from the store avoided the problems of cutting the feed, carrying it across the bay in a boat, maintaining a stable for a winter of six months, milking and churning the pale cream. To people whose all was tied up in precious few possessions, and these maintained from a fund blended of ingenuity and thrift, a cow was a very valuable object. Amid the intimacies that surrounded its necessarily confined winter care, the beast took its place in the functional work-friend relationships that connected the outport dwellers, men and cows alike. And when a cow fell ill, the concern over its health was reinforced by economic factors. And when she had to die, the expertly swung axe was sharpened not only with personal sorrow but also with regret at the loss of four hundred dollars.

Before its euthanasia, however ("easing the poor maid from her torment"), the animal had to contend with a campaign of resuscitation, bleeding, and purging, treatment out of the pages of the eighteenth century. It was partly a wish to do something, to have the sensation of control in an otherwise helpless situation, and partly a modification of the medical inheritance of the early settlers, a mixture of sometimes dubious treatments and folklore. Two hundred years ago, the kings and queens of Europe had the same treatments.

The fact that I was called in to fulfill much the same function as the priest in the human situation underlined the general reaction of distrust toward my outlandish medical imports as an effective curative system. Unless the problem was of the order of the mechanical and straightforward suturing of, say, an udder lacerated by a pack of dogs, I was only beckoned as a last resort. One or two remarkable cures did take place, with all the spontaneity of a veterinary Lourdes, but who can tell whether it was my penicillin or the herb potions of my patients' owners that did the trick? Because such an important possession as a cow was at stake, the use of home remedies – a description that understates their pharmacological ferocity – showed that these remedies were considered worthy of the faith put in them. And the same home remedies were used on people as well. A pragmatic reliance on what was to hand fitted in more with the run of the things than what I had to offer.

And so, with a stained and much-thumbed veterinary manual beside us on the bouncing front seat of the Land Rover, we set off to treat cows.

The first patient was Jerome Rumbolt's cow in Castors River South. Jerome junior reached me at Flower's Cove nursing station by the one and only phone in his settlement.

"I wants the doctor. Doctor speaking? Now, I got a sick cow that ain't gettin' better and I wants for you to take a look at she." Jerome, like most outport Newfoundlanders, treated the telephone as a hostile intermediary and delivered his message staccato, as if he was dictating a telegram over the noise of a crowded room. I knew better by then than to judge him by his abruptness; he was probably a very nice man. I asked what was the matter with the cow.

"We says it's all gall but she's wonderful weak, Doctor, and the skipper thinks we be handy on losing her. And she ain't pissed since morning, neither. Urine, you calls it."

So, half on an errand of mercy and half in the spirit of the new experience, we slithered and ground down the muddy strip of a road for the fifty miles to Castors River South. It looked a poor community, and the little squat frame houses looked extra dismal in the drizzle that hung in the jaundiced glow of the paraffin lights showing at several windows. Jerome Rumbolt senior was both projectionist and owner of a movie house he had built backing onto his cowshed, and, as his son led us in the dark to the cowshed, balancing on planks laid on the quagmire path, we could hear the sounds of cowboys and Indians in pitched battle, whooping and gunfire and a cavalry bugle. Once inside in the light, we were suddenly in a different world.

In the shadowy stalls were three cows, two of them with small calves, and the third, our patient, lying down nearest the door, her legs stretched away from us. The warm, dry air was pregnant with the smells of sudsy milk and hay, and the scene had all the allegorical peace of Bethlehem. It struck me all the more because not for a year had I been so far from the neuroses of the sea.

The sick cow, draped with a strip of canvas, tried to stand and finally managed it with some gentle booting from Jerome. He watched me carefully as I applied my medical techniques in a faltering way, daunted as much by the hairiness of my subject as by her size. The cow was ready to calve and had had some contractions the previous day, which later stopped. I could not hear a fetal heart. Under the canvas I discovered slabs of slated codfish pressed to her back "to keep her kidneys warm with the pickle." The previous day's treatment – pouring several gallons of a purgative brew down her throat and force-feeding her like a Perigourdine goose – had produced no urine, and my attempts to catheterize her using the nursing station stomach-pump tube ended in failure. I felt committed to a pelvic examination and began it with the animal once more lying on her side. Jerome touchingly rolled up my sleeve for me when I found the length of arm I had bared was not nearly enough. My journey to the centre of the cow took me almost to my shoulder joint, and there, in the deepest recesses, I felt something hard and wondered if this was one of the dead calf's feet. But then I worked my fingers above it and found I could pull it out; it looked and smelled like a partly diced onion. Jerome saw my surprise.

"That's the onion Dad put to make her piss."

With a final diagnosis of "yumonie" (pneumonia), we went into Jerome's kitchen, where everyone seemed to have congregated after the movie ended. The room fell silent and I washed my hands and sticky right arm with thirty pairs of eyes on my every move, but the chatter and "rampsing" started up again as I went into the corner by the stove with both Jerome junior and senior to discuss diagnosis, management, and prognosis.

"I ain't certain it ain't the gall after all that," said another man who had joined us.

"But, Doctor, it was civil of ye coming, all the same," said Rumbolt senior, and he meant it.

The second patient belonged to a man called Reuben who lived in one of the communities on the shore of Pistolet Bay in the extreme north of Newfoundland. For all the world, Reuben might have been on a Sunday afternoon drive with his wife and eight children and their friends. He stopped his big Chevy beside me as I walked down the road past the hospital in St. Anthony and asked me did I know a man who could take a look at his cow. A doctor. I got in the car, sitting half on the bony lap of one of his adolescent daughters, and we drove off to the field.

There were several cows on the scrap of exposed pasture which was boggy at one end and sparse at the other, but the sick one singled itself out by its agitated behaviour, coming to us and shaking and wagging its rear end like a swan entering water.

"You'll be all right now, maid, it's the doctor come to see you," said Reuben to his cow, and to me he explained that he thought there was a stoppage in the bowels and that he didn't know whether to kill her or wait to see if she would get better.

"Sure, that's a lot of meat to leave go waste."

Reuben's diagnosis of intestinal obstruction was accurate. The animal's abdomen was slightly swollen and it seethed with visible peristalsis as if full of pythons in extremis. No harm in trying to relieve it, I thought, and by chance Reuben knew where he might put his hand to a length of hose. About eighteen feet of the pipe was washed in the stream and greased with soap, after which I inserted it into the appropriate orifice. Reuben held the other end, supporting it, waiting in a slightly doubtful manner. Six feet had gone inside, and still nothing had happened. Another foot, and then another. Suddenly the cow, who was standing shivering but was nevertheless co-operative, lurched forward a pace, and Reuben, his eye still glued to the spurting hose pipe, shouted, "That's it! My, oh my, oh my. There she blows!" As the green, disgusting evidence of our success spluttered out under enormous pressure over Reuben's head and shoulders, I felt that my medical education had for once proved its full worth.

THE MV *STRATHCONA III*

I used to stand on the hill over Back Cove, look eastward across the Atlantic, and wag my finger at England. I felt myself to be on safe ground to admonish my own country for its complacency and greedy indifference to its affluence. Not only had I been a servant of the welfare state, and knew a little of the misused buffer against suffering that only a rich country can provide, but also, since my arrival in the north of Newfoundland, I had met people for whom that protection was a recent and precious luxury. Until Wilfred Grenfell appeared on the scene in Labrador, most people there had never seen a doctor, knew nothing of the reality of constant access to medicine; for them, disease, especially tuberculosis, was a common event, dreaded yet accepted as another of the burdens of a hard life. At first, before I had seen something of the country, it was difficult to begin to imagine the feelings of a family faced with illness, with no possibility of advice or help, and the dawning certainty of death in their midst.

The situation was no different from more primitive parts of Europe a century ago, but it must be realized that the recent cruel predicament of the Newfoundlander was in parallel to affluence elsewhere. The stories of women dying unrelieved in obstructed labour, of the man who put his mother's corpse on the dog feed scaffold, safely away from the wolves, to await the preacher, of accidents that led unnecessarily to disfigurement or death, of brothers and sisters dying of pneumonia, of poorly managed chronic disease, were commonplace, mostly factual, and told with a shy indifference and fatalism. They are contemporary history, part of the unbuffered suffering of people alive now.

Because of the nature of the outports then – small, unconnected by roads, and mostly without telephones – the usual mechanisms of providing primary health care were not possible. For example, there could not be a doctor or a nurse in each small community. For day-to-day care, especially in the non-roaded areas, we left a box of drugs, ointments, and bandages with a responsible person in each community and prescribed either by telephone or by messenger. This was admittedly a meagre access to the possibilities of modern medicine, and to make our service more substantial we had the alternative of either bringing the patient to St. Anthony or taking hospital facilities to the outports.

It was self-evident that anyone with life-threatening illness, or a condition such as a fracture or acute psychiatric disease that could lead to irreparable complications, should have had immediate access to the base hospital. Yet this apparent right of access to a centralized medical service depended on a costly infrastructure of roads and aircraft services. Before ambulances and helicopters appeared on the scene, the medical services on the Labrador and along the coasts of Northern Newfoundland were necessarily decentralized; the early Grenfell doctors had no choice but to take their hospital facilities to the outports, and the last of the line of the hospital ships, the MV *Strathcona III*, was my home for two summers.

The *Strathcona* was more than a vestigial adjunct to the medical services that were being provided by the hospital at St. Anthony and its efficient, modern transport systems. There were anxious aspects of isolation, many of them concerned with health, that could not be dispelled by the illusory comfort of the availability of an aircraft. Is the child's cough the herald of pneumonia? The old woman has headaches; is she going to get a stroke? His leg is all swelled up – looks poisoned; what if they have to amputate it? When the *Strathcona* sailed into the bay, these questions took on less significance; they were about to be answered. The arrival of an aircraft to take someone away was less of a comfort.

I enjoyed my summers on the *Strathcona*. As the doctor to an intensely maritime people, I felt that my credentials were better received because I lived on a boat. When a man told me he had a pain on the starboard side of his head, I accepted his expression of the symptom with less awkwardness than if we had been in a sterile hospital room three hundred miles from home. And I could step ashore and visit his home without the constraint of a waiting aircraft. Above all there was time to get to know people, both the outport men and women, and the crew of the ship. The *Strathcona*'s skipper, the engineer, and the four crewmen came from the coast and, thanks to them, I learned a lot about my work; of all the healthy Newfoundlanders I met, I got to know them best.

The *Strathcona III* was nearly a hundred feet in overall length, shoal-drafted for the shallow bays and tending to roll in a beam sea; but with her high bow and sheer, she was a good sea boat – as she often had to be. Her medical complements were one or two nurses, an X-ray technician, an occasional dentist, and a doctor. The facilities consisted of a surgery, a dispensary, a small ward, a dental room, and an X-ray room.

The first trip of the summer was to White Bay, up the east coast to the Northern Peninsula of Newfoundland. For five hours we steamed past coastline we knew, past Back Cove in the icy dawn, then Goose Cove Head, across Hare Bay to Commander Island and Fishot; then by St. Julian and Grandois to Croque, into the lee of Groais Island, past Crouse, and on to Conche. It was called the French Shore, the last foothold of the French fishing communities that had stayed since Cartier's discoveries in the early sixteenth century. There were no French left, although some of the very old people could remember the last of them.

Fjord-like gaps in the cliffs gave us glimpses of clustered wooden houses, smoke rising, white trap boats riding at the stages, secret places that the world did not know of, and that, in turn, were mostly happy to leave the world alone. The second engineer and the cook, their breath rising visibly on the frosty breeze, standing in the bows muffled in their parkas, shouted hallo to a fisherman on the way back from his salmon nets. Although the wind had been blowing freshly for a week or more out of the northeast, there was very little swell. I was told that it was being kept in check by a massive icefield out to sea. The last of the swell had helped me to keep down my lunch of fish and brewis. On the first trip the previous year, I had been sick and suffered the agony of wounds to my gullet caused by fishbones going down, and then coming back.

The cook saw a flock of turrs on the water and rushed to the X-ray room where he kept his gun. Too late for that batch, he shot a fulmar in mid-flight for consolation. Unfortunately, such callous acts involving animals were so much a part of the Newfoundland scene that I had ceased to be annoyed by them. Sportsmanship in the accepted, Western, sense did not exist, and had not developed in a land where to eat fresh meat one had first to kill it; and there was such a plethora of wildlife, in and above and beside the sea, that the taking of any individual must have seemed to the Newfoundlander of no more significance than the casual picking of an apple in a great orchard. We sailed by the fulmar that was struggling in the water, mortally wounded.

We were called by the radio telephone operator in St. Anthony, who told us that the nurse in Roddickton had a case needing to see a doctor. Reception was infuriatingly bad, but we thought we were being asked to alter course to Englee, which is on the coast twelve miles from Roddickton. I could not make out what the patient was suffering from, nor could I get an idea from the nurse's controlled R/T voice how bad the condition was. The nurse from Flower's Cove joined in the three-cornered talk and managed to relay the message clearly. As she spoke, I could hear a baby screaming in the background and remembered that a pediatrician was holding clinics at Flower's Cove; the screaming was probably the combined voices of sixty babies. The nurse in Forteau, hearing me on the radio telephone, called up the *Strathcona* and asked for advice on how to treat a woman who had developed pain and blindness in one eye. The airplane had gone to pick up new staff in Gander and was not available for patient transfer that day.

As we changed course to Englee, the nurse in Port Saunders called up Flower's Cove to say she had sent a young girl in labour down the road to St. Anthony, and to give a friendly warning that they might want some help if things started popping in the ambulance on the way past Flower's Cove. And the janitor of the nursing station at Harbour Deep called us to say the nurse there had gone in a hurry to an emergency at the whaling station at Williamsport and would not be there to meet us when we arrived. As we entered the back harbour at Englee, the radio waves fell silent again, and all the routine medical chatter fell out of the ether above the Grenfell Mission like spent fireworks.

There was ice aground in the harbour and the skipper waited near it, keeping his station with occasional use of the engine until a boat was seen coming toward us. Jane Fancott, the nurse from Roddickton, waved to us from the boat, her other arm around the shoulders of a girl aged about seventeen.

I knew the girl, but she was now so ill that she made no sign that she remembered me. I had seen her several times throughout the winter, on the first occasion in her home, when she was bleeding heavily with an abortion at the twelfth week of a pregnancy that she had not been aware existed. The other times were for chest infections and asthma, from which she was suffering now. She came from one of the poorest families, her father being unable to work in the lumber woods due to the consequences of tuberculosis, and her mother, a fat, talkative, slightly belligerent woman, being a bad manager. The girl's clothes were thin and, in spite of a pathetic attempt at the catalogue style of fashion, had a handed-down look about them. She was exhausted by her condition, which had lasted two days in this acute form, and was now shivering with cold and nervousness, unable to talk. She sat on the examination couch in the *Strathcona*'s warm clinic, leaning forward at me, taking her weight on her hands and looking at me with wide, dark eyes that were begging for relief from the torment of breathlessness. The nurse undressed her so that I could examine her, and with automatic modesty she covered up her thin, bony chest with her arms. I had to wait for the ship's engine to die down from a burst before I could listen to the heaving chest.

This is what we had come for, why the *Strathcona* left her snug berth before the dawn, had broken and steamed for five hours down a wild, chilly shore: to let little sounds pass down the tube of a stethoscope, concentrating themselves in my mind, linking perception to scientific methodology and short-circuiting all the other senses. For a moment, unaware of the *Strathcona* rocking gently behind Englee Island, I was in contact with the juicy, taut fabric of troubled lungs, building a diagnosis with bricks of rales (rattling sounds), bronchial fremitus, and resonance.

We decided to take the girl with us, planning to deliver her home on our way back north, or to St. Anthony by airplane should she worsen. As the *Strathcona* got under way, we took specimens of sputum for culture and later examination for the bacilli of tuberculosis. The girl was dehydrated and needed an intravenous infusion; and while we set it up, we took blood for a hemoglobin estimation and gave her aminophylline intravenously to help her tortured breathing. Then we gave her oxygen through the boat's tattered mask and an injection of valium to ease the anxiety that, in spite of our efforts, was still throttling her. Across her chart from the nursing station at Roddickton was written SENSITIVE TO PENICILLIN. She was very ill and should have had an antibiotic as soon as possible, but her sensitivity limited her to tetracycline, the only broad-spectrum antibiotic we were carrying on the boat that did not contain penicillin. By the time we had finished the work – the girl, if not objectively better, at least feeling more comfortable – we were tied up in Harbour Deep.

Harbour Deep was a prototype outport. At our arrival its people came down to the stage, since the coming of *Strathcona* was at least partly a social event; the women, with their sensible coats and shoes and lack of hairdos or cosmetics, looked like country women at market anywhere in the British Isles; the men, tough but mild, looked sure and relaxed on their home ground.

The houses were more than a mile deep in the cleft-like bay and lay higgledy-piggledy on the shore with their backs to a cliff hung with birch and brambles and dogberry. Town planning followed the dictates of geology and the paths between the slabs of granite that supported the seemingly flimsy loads of the frame houses. Foundations were on bedrock, which, usually, was on or near the surface. Around many of the houses were paling fences, each painted the same pastel shade as its house, and beneath some of them lay chained dogs. There was sawdust on the paths to cover the mud, and beyond the settlement the paths led to little gardens, where potatoes were just sprouting.

The settlement had a fishy smell from generations of discarded cod stomachs, but this was laced with a mixture of kelp, tar, and pine sap that made it peculiarly Newfoundlandish. There was no road to Harbour Deep, and no pastor for the church, which was Anglican.

Our equipment, which was stowed for the passage to Harbour Deep, was brought out, and we waited for the nurse's return from Williamsport before we started the clinic; the dentist was already conducting brisk business, his right arm straining, hauling out teeth. A few people had come on board for chest X-rays; although cancer had displaced tuberculosis as the main source of dread, the tubercle bacillus still haunted the folk memory.

By the time the nurse returned, we were eating our evening meal, a real "Jiggs' dinner" of all the possible ingredients of the Newfoundland pot. She had brought back her patient, a man from the south of Newfoundland who had come to work for the summer as a flenser at the Japanese whaling station at Williamsport. He was in acute pain from retention of urine, caused by a urethral stricture stemming from previously untreated gonorrhea, and needed catheterizing. This I did while the nurse warmed herself after her chilly cruise from Williamsport, and had a mug of tea with the *Strathcona's* skipper. I used a large catheter and hoped it would have a dilating effect on the stricture, for the man insisted on returning to work and would not hear of admission to hospital.

Then we started the clinic. The patients came into my office in an order selected by themselves. I knew many of them, mainly the middle-aged, obese women who came along as clinic regulars to have their blood pressure taken.

"I thinks my blood's high, Doctor. It's my youngest maid, out half the night, can't talk to her certainly, she's that contrary. She vexes me, I can't tell no lie. It's so as I can't sleep in the night, wonderful giddy-headed."

The woman's problem lay with obesity as much as with her worries, but it was difficult to evangelize the self-denying aspects of dieting when people were tied by tradition and necessity to potatoes, bread and pies, fatty pork and duck, salt fish (with pork fat) and seal meat (with pork fat): a diet bursting with calories. Eating and the offering of food in a community poor in material gifts was also one of the only means of expressing friendship or obligation. Certainly, to reinforce this observation, I did meet a lot of big, fat women in Harbour Deep.

Raised blood pressure was a common finding in the procession of plump, slightly anxious fishermen's wives. They were sporadic guzzlers of pills given to them at one time or other by doctors and nurses, medication comprising the whole spectrum of the history of the treatment of hypertension. However, such pills did not have any effect on the diet nor on the closed isolation of the communities that gave rise to mental tension, both known causes of high blood pressure.

On the *Strathcona* we were in a good position to investigate other possible remedial aspects of the condition, and to carry out electrocardiography and X-rays, without uprooting people from their homes. In that day's group we found a woman with diabetes and another with ischemic heart disease.

Next there was a young woman in the clinic with her baby son, born in Harbour Deep's nursing station a year ago. She was not sure but she thought he needed circumcising. While I examined him, and we were both focusing down on the child's tiny prepuce, she told me, as if in passing, that she felt "none too good." Shyly, until she overcame her initial nervousness, she told of tiredness and shortness of breath, loss of weight and appetite, all symptoms related to her inability to work and look after her young family. Her monthly periods had stopped but she was sure she was not pregnant.

She was pale, but it was difficult to assess her anemia clinically because she had a low-grade conjunctivitis. There was an ulcer at the left angle of her mouth. She had enlarged glands in her neck and groin. She had a bruise on her left thigh. I thought I could feel the edge of her spleen. A chest X-ray showed masses in the hilar lymph node area (in the lungs), and there was widening of the abdominal aorta. We took blood for a smear and for a hemoglobin estimation. I did a rather inexpert stain on the smear and looked down the microscope onto a galaxy of abnormal white blood cells.

The girl, who had busied herself wrapping her baby in

his blanket, knew something was wrong, accepted in silence
that she would have to go to the hospital at St. Anthony "for
tests." She had a brief try at putting it off; could she go when
the salmon was over? Then her man would be able to see to the
crowd at home. She quietly argued over details with the nurse,
as though her subconscious was aware of the prognosis of
acute leukemia, and she knew she had to bargain for as much
time at home as possible. I went aft to the *Strathcona*'s two-bed
ward to see the asthmatic girl. She was sleeping and breathing
more easily, the oxygen mask slipped over one ear.

I took a break, made myself a mug of tea in the galley,
and took it to the bridge; I was anxious to hear the six o'clock
scheduled radio contact with the hospital, in order to find out
what the airplane was doing the next day. People were still
coming down to the wharf, and the clinic would go on into the
evening. A fisherman had just come back with a codfish that
he had jigged just outside the bay, and the interest in his catch
was great; it is like prospectors who hope that a nugget will
lead to a seam. In very few places in the world could the sight
of a fish produce so much excitement. The outports were truly
built on a foundation of cod stomachs.

I thought the next patient, a girl of three, brought because
of bad warts on her hands, was Inuit. Her darkish skin, her
facial structure with high, wide cheekbones and slanted
eyes, and her dark fringe of hair marked her as one, and the
race was recently familiar to me. But her young mother and

grandmother, with their auburn curls and their freckled complexions, were as Irish as could be. The nurse explained the mystery afterward. The father of the child was Japanese, one of the managers of the whaling station. It seemed that, by some genetic alchemy, through the mixing of Japanese and Celtic blood, a perfect Inuk had been created. While pondering on this, I cauterized the warts with a silver nitrate stick.

The clinic continued with its usual assortment of men with bad necks, usually with no objective signs to pinpoint any lesion but real enough to the sufferer, and women with urinary tract infections. The men could go on welfare, but the women had to soldier on with the scant comfort of a sulpha drug.

I was aware that we were offering an imperfect service, that we were hardly touching the problems of chronic disease in an isolated place. But at the same time I felt that the people of Harbour Deep were sleeping a little bit sounder while the *Strathcona* was tied up at their wharf, and late that night, sitting in my bunk with its view down the long, starlit fjord, I was glad that I had been able to play some part in that peace of mind.

THE FALL OF THE YEAR

To the Northern Newfoundlander, the fall of the year was the time in which he had to metamorphose from a summer to a winter man. It was the span of time between activity of the summer and the enforced idleness of the winter, a period of adaptation, often much taken up with domestic affairs, an annual retirement. The money had been made and the winter stores ordered, the decision taken whether or not to build another boat. The days were often warm and balmy, and it was often difficult to feel detached from the summer; more so if there were still signs of fish because the boats remained in the water.

It was then that the schoolteachers came down from the south, swept out the schools in the winter settlements, and lit the stoves to dry out books and boxes of chalk. Wintry winds were stalking down the Labrador Current, and soon they would molest the fishing outports, built as they were on the shelterless Atlantic shore, on the "outside." Everyone would "shift in" to the winter settlements, the boats piled high with bedding, pots and pans, dogs and children, a journey to the far end of the bay, where there was shelter and trees for firewood and building. By the time school started, the "outside" was abandoned to the winter.

There is no outstanding feature of the Newfoundland autumn, no blazing foliage or drifts of crispy leaves. The temptation is not to think of autumn as a season at all and to look instead for signs of the approaching winter, the first really cold day, the first batch of steady north winds, but to do so is to be unaware of its value. Autumn is the only time of year when the treadmill of the seasons is out of gear; freeze-up, winter gales, blizzards, frost, breakup, pack ice, fog, and icebergs are all in the past, or yet to come. The fall of the year is a time for taking stock.

Conche, September

I am lying in long grass at Cape Fox, Conche, looking out to the Grey Islands. The Horse Islands are just visible, far to the south on a clear horizon. I have brought about twenty children with me for the walk from Conche, and they call the Horse Islands the "Arse" Islands, intending no disrespect in their innocent minds. It is a day for sunbathing and we are all in shirtsleeves – rare for this country – and for some of us our undressing is far more advanced than shirtsleeves. A minute ago I was fighting with one brawny future fisherman, aged five, and he squirmed away leaving most of what he was wearing in my hands. One group is gathering berries that they then place in my wide-open mouth. Three girls scramble down into a small cove where they find the ground raspberries that they call "plumboys." A small boy with wire-rimmed, pebble spectacles has a private patch of bakeapples some distance away that he guards jealously and picks at myopically like a pigeon, jerking his head back to spy out the next one. Some are specialists in blackberries and others in blueberries, sweeter and juicier, that they call "hurts." A game begins to see whose aim into my mouth is the best, and I foolishly let it continue until the berries become ammunition in a war for the occupation of Fox Cape.

September 20

Modern whaling is the most businesslike of blood sports, ruthless, organized, and technological. Because it is so effective, the very existence of some species of whale have become endangered, and the disapproval that most people have for killing whales comes after pondering the statistics of diminishing whale numbers. But no one can know how magnificent an animal a whale is until he has seen one. A dead whale especially, freshly killed and hauled from the water, the harpoon's wound in the great chest still pouring blood, feeds one's anti-whaling emotions as no dry statistics can. As one is engulfed by the shadow of the taken whale, the realization comes, with a burst of anger, that it would be a very great pity if the oceans were emptied of them.

We left for Williamsport from Harbour Deep at dawn today, and there was something sinister about the whaling station as we approached it in our small boat. The trip down the coast had been rough and breezy, but the water was still and black in the fjord, little more than a cleft reaching back a mile through the high cliffs, and as we approached the wharf, the stillness was accentuated, made dreamlike as in a painting, by the sharp contrast with our recent buffeting at sea and by the absence of people. On the slip, dwarfing the low, wooden buildings, the engine house, the distillation plant, and the rusty oil storage tanks, was a whale as black as the water it had left forever. The nightmarish, surrealistic effect was increased by the appearance on the scene of a middle-aged Japanese man in a dark lounge suit and white gloves who came down to meet us as we clambered up from our boat.

Thus welcomed by the manager of the whaling station, we were taken inside for a breakfast – not of whale steaks, but of eggs, bacon, and coffee. The clinic that followed did not last long, and when it was over I went outside to take a photograph of the whale. The day had turned warm and the sun was making its short visit to our crack between the rocky heights, glancing reflections of blue skies off the narrow water. What had been in the shadow of darkness was now all colour. The whale's back was being worked on by flensers who let gory slabs of flesh slide down to where men waited with hooks; they in turn passed the slabs on to be cut up and stacked. At least a quarter-acre of cobbled ground was covered by meat, which, in the late-summer sun, was warming up to an indescribable stench and putting frenzy into the flies. In the shock induced by this bombardment of the senses (which, as a doctor, I would have thought might have affected me less) I forgot to take my photograph.

October 15

I left St. Anthony this morning and drove to Port Saunders, going slowly as befitted such a warm, lazy day. The hills of Labrador, which reached to virgin country as far as Alaska, seemed very near and were as optically clear as if the Strait of Belle Isle was a narrow stream. In the flat, barren country below Big Brook, the dusty surface of the road, kicked up by other cars, was like funnels of tornadoes creeping toward me from miles away, and as we passed each other there was a limbo of uncertainty before my Land Rover sped out of the dust into the sunshine again, miraculously still on the road.

Most of the year's work is now over. All along the road I saw men, young working men, out in the sunshine and doing nothing in particular. There were some boats already out of the water, pulled up on the shore, unturned. There were two longliners out, just above Anchor Point. The next source of income will be the netting of salmon in the spring, and for some, earlier next year, the seals. This year has not been a particularly good one, but I think most people have made a living. This is one of the best times of year, with good weather and restful days.

A CLINIC AT RODDICKTON

I was billed to give a clinic at Roddickton; notices had been posted to that effect in the window of Decker's general store and at the post office, and Roddickton's nurse had pointed out to me over the radio telephone that the response to the news of a clinic had been great. It was her way of telling me not to forget to come, to remind me that it was nearly seven weeks since the people of Roddickton last had the chance to see a doctor.

The dirt road to Roddickton was long, its one hundred and fifty bone-shaking, car-breaking miles the very reason why I might have been tempted to "forget" Roddickton, yet once under way I always enjoyed the drive through the wilderness spruce forest. As I neared my destination I was given the final treat of one of those theatrical Newfoundland sunsets, where the clear western sky was suddenly stabbed, and the lifeblood of the day welled up, soaking into small, pretty clouds, spilling over into the ponds, reddening the silver birches and even the face of my watch. I stopped the Land Rover and walked across the road to see the sunset in peace. All along the roadside were rows of neatly stacked logs, and I sat on them in the still, warm dusk before I drove the last few miles to the nursing station.

If there was any money in the pockets and purses of the people of Roddickton it was because of work in the lumber woods. The logs I had sat on to watch the sunset were destined to be pulped, raw material for a rich paper industry, but for all the wealth derived from its pulpwood, Roddickton gave no sign that it had played any part in the chain of affluence. Its member of Newfoundland's provincial assembly was Mr. Edward Roberts, who had come there electioneering, to make promises, and with whom I picked my way along the potholed, muddy paths between the houses. He kept his promises.

No fishermen live in Roddickton; it is twelve miles from the open sea, a scatter of houses at the end of Canada Bay, a base only for the plunder of forests. During the three years I was acquainted with Roddickton, few ships from England or Scandinavia came into the bay to take away the wood. Jobs were always scarce and intermittent and the welfare officer was a busy man. The outside investment that raped the forests brought no mitigation or reforestation schemes, and the knowledge that the lumber woods were not being replenished added to the precarious nature of Roddickton's dependency on the outside world. The fishing communities never had the same dismal air, even when their catches were poor and the price of fish low. The difference was that between the unemployed and the self-employed.

The people who, mostly between the two World Wars, chose to migrate to Roddickton were not of the Irish and French stock who fished on the nearby coast. The names of the woodsmen have an English, non-Celtic ring to them; Canning, Randell, Hancock, Tucker, Pilgrim. The Christian names reflect the fundamentalist Protestant sects of the area: Rebecca, Hezekiah, Levi, Elijah, Moses, Aaron, and Booth.

My Land Rover was a familiar sight as it struggled along the main street in mud up to its axles. By the time I reached the nursing station, ten or more people with suddenly remembered complaints would have telephoned the nurse to make an appointment. The waiting room, which served as both the porch and basement entrance of the station, was already filled with a talkative crowd – the usual cross-section of the town. They seemed to be enjoying themselves, and, as usual, the clinic had its social overtones, that atmosphere being one of disciplined hilarity, like a church picnic. They brought with them the smell of the houses, a mixture of woodsmoke and a sweet, human odour that was a product of a lack of running water and poor sanitary arrangements. The men rolled thin cigarettes and smoked them to the very end, the podgy babies sported and bubbled on broad, threadbare laps, knocking over their bottles that smashed onto the concrete floor, while their mothers gossiped in a forthright manner, eighteenth-century words and syntax adorning the swirl of their raucous voices like ripe fruit.

As I waited for the first patient to come in, I was very conscious that the door to the clinic separated two centuries. On my side were technology and a representative experience of modern Europe, and on theirs, the survival of a transplant from a Europe that had been left behind. I felt that it was easier to go into the future than to trespass in the past. As they came through my door, they adapted to my twentieth-century imports with much greater ease than I would have found had I gone to live amongst them. I put great value on their qualities of kindness and charity, and saw some of my own identity in their obvious roots in a European culture familiar to me. But sadly, my education separated me from them, putting my perception at an irrevocably different level to theirs. The confusion lay in our common language that had at first lulled me into overlooking the gulf of experience between us.

My greatest difficulty was with the accurate translation of their conceptions of anatomy and physiology into the rigid classifications of medicine's language. Their ideas about their own bodies were culled from a mixture of folklore and innocent speculation. There was no health education in Roddickton, and the doctors who came to hold clinics were always too busy to be teachers. Consequently the symptoms that were presented were never the logical expression of an ordered pathology, but instead were based on a special logic, often bizarre and peculiar to each individual.

A strongly built woman with a black dress way down below her knees, and an acre of lap, came into the clinic. She sat in front of me with the expression of one waiting to go on stage, burdened by her lines. A large baby was making heavy going of pushups on her knees, and her shy gaze darted between the baby, the nurse, and me as she waited for her cue to begin her story. She came from a nearby Apostolic community and wore her hair in the loose bun known locally as an apostolic roll. She was not a regular attender at the nursing station, and the journey from her home would have been expensive for her.

"It's the little fella, Doctor, he's getting awful choked up on his stomach, on times, can't scarce seem to catch his wind. My, I gets some scared up watching him. And cough, coughing half the night. And his water goes weak, Doctor, and his poor little bird goes right blue certainly, and him rubbing on his poll, Doctor, I'm certain he finds his little poll. And I gets scared half to death, that his insides is all twisted up cause he gets sick to his stomach something shocking. Doctor, we was wondering if you has some kind of tonic or a penicillin needle could help his blackouts?"

It was difficult to persuade her that her baby was all right, merely too fat; and then I felt that she was not at all persuaded but had only paused to argue for her point of views. Her stern silence did not mean a victory for medical common sense.

Mine taught that obesity was connected with respiratory disease, with a lowered resistance to infection, and a baby's rate of development; hers said that plumpness was a sign of robustness and of her own good care. She wanted me to cure her baby of a dramatic-seeming syndrome I could neither name nor describe in terms of the medicine I had been taught.

I examined the infant carefully and, finding it to be a healthy specimen, I bridged the gap between our cultures with a sedative, brightly coloured, in what was an almost homeopathic dose; the mother would have benefited more from it than the baby. I was annoyed at having been pressured into giving something (she would never have accepted advice without a bottle of medicine). She was annoyed that her story had fallen flat and that I seemed continually to change the subject from her baby's "disease" to my strange ideas and had failed to concentrate on what she was saying. I hoped as she left that she would change his diet a little and let him breathe some fresh air, but felt that would be the last time she would bring him to my clinics and that she might even avoid medicine altogether in future, availing herself instead of the alternatives provided by the Apostolics.

Naturally enough, when there were physical signs to be seen, the symptoms made more sense, even if they were presented on an odd systematic basis. And as most of the patients were suffering from infections of one sort or another, such signs were generally present.

Like any good culture medium, Roddickton was a reservoir for germs, which it incubated in its warm, crowded kitchens and well-populated beds. Much of the work of the clinics was always concerned with the ravages of bacteria, either directly, with acute infections and abscesses, or obliquely, with illnesses caused by the scarring that follows past infection. That evening in Roddickton I saw a child with a "gathered" ear, that is, a discharging otitis media, and a dark-complexioned, Indian-looking girl with a "raised throat" (tonsillitis). The tonsillitis had given rise to a quinsy, which luckily burst when she gargled with brine so that I did not have to lance it. I saw a procession of obese, sweating babies in arms who spent their lives – until liberated by learning to walk – lying, wrapped in blankets in front of kitchen stoves, with varying degrees of chest infections. Two of them were serious enough to admit to the station; one looked as if it would expire at any moment, requiring oxygen and a drip. Luckily, the local germs lacked the sophistication of hospital germs and usually succumbed to the common antibiotics we had in stock.

Another girl, pale and pinched, her hair in curlers under a scarf, came in with a transmitted affliction of an entirely different sort, and she shyly gave us the clue to the diagnosis.

"I come to see if I got to get married", she said. "I wants you to make a test on my water."

The specimen, in a plastic shampoo bottle with oily blobs of shampoo floating on the surface, was produced, wrapped discreetly in a brown paper bag. She did indeed have to get married. On pelvic examination I could feel her uterus at about twelve weeks of gestation, and we dispelled the situation of its naïveté even further by taking a specimen of blood, for grouping and a hemoglobin estimation, and booking her in the usual routine of the station.

Late in the evening, the routine of the clinic was punctuated with a little grim relief when some men arrived with one of their comrades: he had "got his back broke in the lumber woods–a big stick falled on him and caught him across the lungs." The man had been unconscious, although he was now coming round a little, and the reflexes of his lower limbs were brisk: an indication of possible damage to his spinal cord. The accident had happened late in the afternoon, not far from the place I had sat to watch the sunset, but it had been some time before he had been found and the tree could be pried off him. His friends had carried him most of the two miles, sure he was dying, or even dead, a stumbling cortège along the banks of a brook, and one of them had run on ahead to arrange to have a truck waiting at the road.

As consciousness returned he was in obvious pain and, after I made sure he had no signs of a head injury that would have been masked by an opiate, we gave him an injection of morphine. There was marked swelling and small lacerations over his lower ribs and spine, and it seemed certain that there were fractures of the ribs on both sides as well as the lower thoracic and upper lumbar vertebrae. With such a great degree of skeletal, and possibly neurological, injury he would have to go to hospital, and we sent word to Roddickton's bus driver that there was a patient for the trip to St. Anthony.

I set up an intravenous infusion on the injured man and examined his abdomen to see if he had ruptured his spleen or other viscera. We left some clothes on him for the journey north, and it was only by chance, when he cried out as we lifted him onto the stretcher, that I decided to examine him further and found that he had fractured his right humerus. We were fixing the splint when the bus, converted to an ambulance by putting a mattress on its floor, arrived at the station.

I often wondered if the Newfoundlanders were less susceptible to pain than most people or whether they merely had a more stoical attitude to it. Some groups, notably the French in my experience, have a fatalistic approach to their own death, and it is a quality shared by the Newfoundlanders, but they took it further; their fatalism encompassed physical as well as mental suffering. The modality of pain feeds on imagination and emotion, and the Newfoundlander has these qualities as much as any man, reacting to pain in others with compassion and tender action. Yet, from my point of view, he or she was able to keep still, to keep alert, to remain cheerful and co-operative, long after his contemporary of another nationality would have lost control. An analogy that suggests itself is that of the crews of the eighteenth-century

Ship of the Line, who faced appalling injury and barbaric surgery and lived to describe exactly what had happened to them. The analogy holds up well when one considers how the people looked, talked, and behaved. Four generations of the availability of anaesthetics have numbed the capability of most Western men and women to react to pain calmly and with dignity. Mercifully, pain is no longer part of the daily scene, but it continues to lurk in the wings, coming to seem more and more terrible, and will continue to do so for as long as people have bodies. Women are better equipped than men, perhaps because they have been inoculated against the fear of pain by the actuality of childbirth, and the stoicism of many women around the world parallels the average bravery of the Newfoundlander.

The ambulance came and went, and the crowded clinic at Roddickton gave no indication that we would go to bed at all that night. The waiting room, lit by one naked bulb, remained as full as ever, no one believing that the doctor would still be around the next day, and everyone determined to make use of me while there was a chance. It felt odd to be treated like a windfall that might be snatched away at any moment, and it was this sensation of being valuable that allowed me to remain enthusiastic amid a seemingly endless stream of routine medical problems. Roddickton gave a fillip to drudgery.

SOME REFLECTIONS, AND A
LITTLE HISTORY

Very few people of my generation, which is the one born in the 1939 to 1945 war period, have the experience of entering a foreign country by any route other than the normal one. With our vital passports crammed with visas, we have freedom to jostle from one frontier to another in full view of customs, immigration, health and police authorities, controlled and confined. And when I encountered the Labrador Coast, two years after my medical service with the Grenfell Mission, this was my first landfall after a voyage across the Atlantic in a small sailing yacht. It felt odd to step ashore on the new-found-land, unwelcomed by any bureaucracy, strange not to be added to a list.

A landfall after a long sea voyage, especially in a small boat where there may at times have been doubt as to the outcome, has many qualities of a magical event. It is anticipated, yet surprises, and involves an element of rebirth. My voyage, planned as a repetition of the Viking trading routes between Europe and North America, also allowed me to visit that part of the northeastern Canadian coast where I had worked two years previously as a doctor. And so it was that coming ashore on the Labrador Coast allowed me to see familiar people and places with new eyes.

With my mind freed for a while from the pressures of civilization, and geared to the rhythms of the sea, I approached the country this time with a degree of innocence, with a glimmer of the insight that an early settler might have had. The land was harsh-looking, rocky and treeless, but worked into deep bays that gave shelter from the infinitely harsher sea. It was still possible to catch a ten-pound codfish within two minutes with an unbaited hook. The welcome from people who lived in the bays was spontaneous and undemanding, unexpected like a delicious fruit from that barren place. This time round I was an illegal arrival, immediately accepted, and if I had been prepared to work at the fish, I could have stayed safely forever. In that sense not much had changed in three hundred years.

Four years previously, I had answered an advertisement in the *British Medical Journal* for the appointment of "a travelling doctor with the Grenfell Mission, with interesting and varied work in Subarctic." I was at the crossroads, two years after qualifying, of wondering whether to specialize in medicine, as my father had done, or go into general practice, and that advertisement was a subtle signpost for general practice. I applied for the job and was accepted and, a month later, was in an aircraft on my way to Newfoundland.

During that month, I had resigned from my first job as a medical registrar at a hospital in the East End of London, worked my notice, bought a Land Rover and made arrangements for shipping it to Canada, went through immigration formalities, and prepared lists for packing. But as I sat in the Air Canada jet I realized that in the rush I had had no time to find out just what, or where, I was going to. The few enquiries I had made in the Canadian Embassy had revealed little. No one had seemed to know much about that part of their country. In a short search I had found no books on Northern Newfoundland, but I did manage to buy a detailed map.

I felt like a participant in an arranged marriage; all I had were some names from the map, a lot of preconceptions, jumbled with emotions as I left my familiar country, and a mixture of excitement and apprehension. There was also loneliness that seemed to match my first sighting of the land as the airplane descended for the final approach; the country was flat, barren, and empty, with scrappy patches of early winter snow overlapping bent-over purples and greens. The preconceptions had peopled the island with folk blended from Thomas Hardy and Jack London, from Wild West and gold rush mythologies, and from my own wishful thinking, and they were given substance by the names. My map had each of the fissures of an indented coast labelled with a name that was almost a description in itself, and with the island of Newfoundland in my sights for the first time, the names began to give personalities to my imaginary people: Heart's Delight, Come by Chance, George's Cove, Deadman's Cove, Little Harbour Deep, Ireland's Bight, Baccalieu, Fogo, Funk. But the names were real enough and my first clue to the character of an elusive people.

Newfoundland is the easternmost province of Canada, and its capital, St. John's, is as near to Ireland as it is to Montreal, some would say in temperament as well as distance. The main bulk of the island lies in the south, but it sends a peninsula northward to the fifty-second parallel, a finger to test the coldness of the Labrador Current, that almost touches the coast of the Labrador.

It was across the top half of this peninsula that I worked, on a line northward from Harbour Deep on the Atlantic side, around the tip of the Northern Peninsula, and south to the River of Ponds on the Strait of Belle Isle side, as well as along the coast of Southern Labrador from L'Anse au Clair to Port Hope Simpson. Five hundred odd miles of coastline, with less than half of it in contact by road with the base hospital in St. Anthony, and with twenty thousand patients, may seem an impossible situation for a general practice, but there were mitigating circumstances that on balance gave the people a better medical service than obtained in places considered to be more sophisticated.

In the main centres of population, small clinics had been set up which were run by nurses who worked as general practitioners, with freedom to treat patients as they saw fit, and ease of referral by aircraft or road for the acutely ill or any diagnostic problem. There were seven of these clinics, called nursing stations, and it was in or from these I worked. I saw any problem of diagnostics or treatment that, in medical parlance, the nurses considered "cold" enough to await my arrival, and I visited each nursing station once every four to six weeks, and so for most of the time, as far as each nurse was concerned, I was somewhere else. Where there were roads, and elsewhere with a bush-flying aircraft on floats or skis constantly in commission, they managed perfectly well without me, and this access to a well-endowed base hospital made me entirely dispensable.

The very real value of my job was to bring a sense of security to mostly healthy people by showing them, in an isolated situation, that there were doctors on hand. The fact was that I was kept busy most of the time, there was always a welcome for me in the nursing stations, and the nurses were always glad of a second opinion amid the constant pressure of work. The combination of my usefulness and a natural fascination for the area produced much of what I believe is job satisfaction, but there were other ingredients that enriched the equation. From the vantage point of medical practice, I had the chance to see people who were poignantly at the end of an era, teetering unknowingly at the edge of new things. In my memory this is what added fat to the gravy.

The outside world was encroaching for the first time on the isolation of the northern communities, and their own government was trying to make sense of their future with resettlement programs and social welfare policies. As a doctor, often dependent on my hosts, it was natural for me to be present at family discussions as long-standing communities broke up. I saw the result of building a road to an outport (the term I like best for the isolated village-like communities) that had been for three centuries without one. I was there to see telephones installed that ended isolation for the first time. I had as my contemporaries the first entirely literate generation. Canadians that I have met doing voluntary work in other countries of the world have expressed great surprise when I have told them of conditions in one part of their own country. And there are some Newfoundlanders who have forgotten their origins in the outports, and who might even be offended to be considered in the same light as the outport men and women. But in these pages the description of the Newfoundlander (pronounced "noofndlander") is restricted to the twenty thousand people on the coastline that I travelled along and is meant to do the opposite of giving offence.

As I travelled from place to place for my clinics, which

were often held in one of the homes of a community or in the essentially homey atmosphere of a nursing station, the nature of the job freed me from all the mental barriers that people erect to deal with the spectre of hospitals. On the other hand, the difficulty of making worthwhile relationships with my patients was made hard enough by personal and cultural barriers. Even by the end of my stay, despite the many friendships that developed among naturally generous and friendly people, I was still regarded as, and treated like, a stranger.

The outport men and women show great reserve to strangers, which is a natural expression of the wariness of early settlers who were refugees of a harsh bureaucracy. This distrust stems from times when strangers almost always were dangerous: revenue officers and other agents of authority who through repression had caused the migration of the outport people into their secret bays in the first place.

Nowadays, with welfare cheques, family allowances, fishermen's stamps, and pensions, this bogeyman has ceased to exist, and has passed into ethnic consciousness as the janny or the mummer, or plain Old Nick. Even so, he lives on as a legacy from harder times, embodied in a modern type of stranger who is not obviously threatening, and who is only a stranger because he does not "belong to the place" in the sense that he was not born there. This includes men who have married into the communities from the outside, as well as welfare officers, policemen, doctors, and teachers. For generations there has been no standard of comparison with the outside world and easy hospitality can be beset by an uneasy mind.

The mentality of the fugitive is still a strong factor in outport life. It has been suggested that the evolutionary purpose for its survival has been to divert aggressive feelings away from the community by pinning them on an outside agent. A knock on the door means someone is outside who does not know he has no need to knock to come in. I was usually taken to an inner part of the house, possibly never seen by some of the people "who belonged" in the community; the kitchen was the natural forum, and only strangers were taken farther. A father, instead of directly confronting a naughty child, would knock loudly on the wall, making believe it was the nurse outside wanting to take the child away. The mummers came barging in at Christmastime and defused the most explosive time of year. In small, isolated communities aggression could otherwise have been a destructive force, and I saw it in this role once or twice, especially in the marooning winter months when travel was disrupted and there was little to do. In the closed, closely related outports the stranger has developed a scapegoat function.

However, strangers, in a part of the world without any tourism, have to be looked after, for they would otherwise perish in the harsh climate, and natural suspicion is balanced against natural kindness. The result is that the Newfoundlander has learned to act the fool. He has suffered too much to let down his guard completely.

But at least I was free of the millstone of hospitals. I once met a man of about sixty who had brought himself to the modern hospital at St. Anthony by boat – possibly the first time he had left his bay in his life. He was walking backward in circles, clutching his old hat before him in the position of reverence. The antiseptic smell, the nurses, pumiced and businesslike, dressed in unblemished white, the atmosphere of impersonal purpose, was making a great impression on him. He could not see how he fitted into it at all; a little, bowed man with dirty, patched clothes smelling of fish and woodsmoke.

In his home I was the stranger, the man to be carefully offered comfort and help. It made the possibility of a relationship easier, if only just. And when he fell ill, his approach to me, whatever his outward manner of indifference or reserve, confidence or belligerence, was one of vulnerability, and, for our relationship to be effective, this had to be converted into trust. In a sense, therefore, a by-product of my job was the privilege of glimpses behind the guard of the Newfoundlander, and it is of these that this book is a blow-by-blow account.

The Newfoundlanders who were my patients were descendants of west of England and Irish settlers. They spoke a lively English that conjured up the past. Their genetic inheritance was mainly from the European settlers, but there was a scant admixture from the Inuit and the North American Indian. Many of their settlements had French names.

The mainstream of Newfoundland and Labrador history is well-charted, from discovery and recorded colonization and exploitation, through a series of treaties and haggles between England and France, the other claimant of the island, to confederation with Canada in 1949. But beside the main channel, the shifting sands of individual motive and personal history are less well marked, partly through the low educational priorities of the early settlers and their descendants, and partly from an understandable disinclination to tell the truth to official enquirers. And the facts that were recorded by these early officials were possibly compiled into reports that would please higher official ears. Administrators would tell of successful battles against lawlessness against all the odds, educated travellers would dwell on the picturesque or poignant, and the clergy emphasized the widespread depravity as a lever for more money for their churches. With the secretive people, truth is always harder to come by.

The earliest humans to hunt through the forests and coasts of Newfoundland and Labrador were tribes of Beothuk, and Micmac (Mi'kmaq) Indians, the Nascopie and Montagnais Indians (Innu), and the Eskimo (Inuit). Archaeologists have also found earlier, cultural variants of the present-day Inuit, Innu, and Beothuk. Except for the Inuit, many of these people focused on the woods and interior rivers for their living, and somewhat less on the sea; yet it was the sea whose tremendous fertility was to attract the fishing fleets and the men from

Europe, and bring about the eventual extermination of the Beothuk.

The lives of these indigenous peoples remained unknown to the rest of the world until, 800 years before Columbus, a crew of Norsemen led by Bjarni Herjolfsson found their way across the Atlantic and coasted the western shore of the ocean to the wild vineyards of Cape Cod. At the whim of bad weather they had crossed the Atlantic by the Northern Route, by way of Iceland and Greenland, and in crossing the Davis Straits they became the first Europeans to see the coast of Labrador and the New World. It seems likely that the Vikings colonized the new shores, which they called Vinland, and that trade in precious timber developed between colonies and the established, but treeless, settlements in Greenland. If this were so, staging posts in Newfoundland would have been useful to the north- and southbound traffic, and the excavated Viking remains at L'Anse aux Meadows documents one of these ports of call.

As the Vikings declined and were no longer able to guarantee protection and reinforcements to their western outposts, the Norsemen of Vinland moved on or perished, but probably not before mating with Inuit women, as later settlers did, and most likely leaving a genetic legacy of the Norsemen for the new world. It is improbable that over several generations there was not some mixing of races. When I once delivered a baby of a woman who was broad-faced with Inuit features, and the baby was fair-skinned like no one else in the settlement, was the child a Viking infant in my hands, a footnote to the sagas?

The history of Newfoundland from the fifteenth century onward is dominated by a central character: the slippery hero of any story of the island is the codfish, known everywhere as plain "fish" and, after its rediscovery by Europeans, Newfoundland became a factory ship, anchored as if for the use of the fishing fleets of the Grand Banks. For centuries the cod formed the basis of work, reward, food, imagination, chatter, and aspiration; in many places it still does.

A rich source of protein such as the Grand Banks and the inshore waters of Newfoundland was an immediate attraction to the merchants of West Country England, Jersey, Brittany, and the Basque countries, who saw a profit in the harvest of a great crop they would never have to sow. Because the early fleets were seasonal, returning to Europe with their catch, the early settlements failed due to difficulties in administration and the risks of competing with sea-based operations. Nevertheless, the numbers of men and women on the early ships were large enough to ensure that a significant percentage would find their way ashore, either through desertion or illness or in order to maintain the temporary shore bases of the summer fleets. These were the first settlers, unpaid and unprotected, and accountable to no one.

At the time of my work with the International Grenfell Association, there was still a fleet that came from Europe for the summer and fished on the Grand Banks. I have seen the Portuguese schooners stormbound in St. John's harbour and spoken with several of the crews. They climbed into little dories and fished in all sorts of weather, one man to each unstable cockleshell, drifting on the fickle seas of the Grand Banks more than a day from land. On board ship they had cramped quarters and monotonous food, and their lot, although certainly a paradise to their sixteenth and seventeenth-century counterparts, helped me understand the motives of the early settlers who deserted to a country with the prospects of harsh winters and dubious survival. And in the early days there was the double spur of escaping the servitude of a repressed peasantry at home.

After two hundred years the settlers became numerous and were eventually organized by local entrepreneurs, known as planters. Their competition came materially to affect the European investment, and the repression they had known in Europe was suddenly a reality in their new home. However, the new laws making it illegal to settle were unenforceable: the sheltered coves and deep bays to the north provided a refuge not only from the cruel sea but also from detection and punishment. Thus hidden, their eventual diffusion into every tenable nook on the wild way north depended only on the territorial necessity of each man to have enough of the seabed for his primitive fishing methods to yield a living.

By the late seventeenth century a recognizable society

had developed, with no social hierarchy other than the natural divisions caused by ability, existing as pockets of life separated by the headlands of an uncharted coast. There were possibly as many as four thousand people, mostly West Country men, but including groups of French and Irish. They became inshore fishermen, building two homes, one "on the outside" for the summer's fishing and one deep in the bay where there was protection in the hard winters and wood for stoves and for building. As they moved north where the sea froze in the winter, making fishing impossible for half the year, they learned to be hunters and woodsmen, and the new tactics of survival were mirrored in the words that appeared to describe the new world: slob hauler, glitter, bedlamer, komatik.

These men and women, from different backgrounds, religions, and nationalities, composed of uncompromising sects, and often belligerent ethnic personalities, were moulded by identical conditions, salted down by the hard winters and the need to survive. The result was a recognizable Newfoundland stock. From the start they avoided the problems of institutional strife – the hallmark of the social order they had left behind – since the potentially warring groups were kept apart by the policing headlands and there was the necessity to keep the communities small and independent. The English settled apart from the French; the Irish Catholics from the English Protestants. Conche was Catholic; Harbour Deep, Protestant; there were Cornishmen in Bear Cove, and Welshmen in Rexons Cove.

The fabric of the new life contained the additional weave of the Indian and the Inuit, who although displaced by the settlers did not disappear; their ability to survive in the forests, their stealth in hunting, their skill in driving a team of dogs and in coming to terms with the horrors of pack ice, all remained. They left other indications of their tenancy of the island, legacies of complexion and physiognomy, mannerism and philosophy, which became other facets of the outport mould.

Without the benefits of technology, for the Northern Newfoundlander never knew of an industrial revolution, there was only one way to deal efficiently with his surroundings, and that way became the norm for the northern outports. It had to be evolved within one generation, or the next would not have survived, and it remains today in many places just as it was created: a rough and steady application of seaman-like self-reliance and common sense. The way of life and the mental equipment necessary to it are not learned by rote, but rather absorbed from the air laden with the smell of fish, tarred twine, and woodsmoke, or soaked into the skin from a poultice of sodden clothes after a day jigging for fish. The Newfoundlander had an identity and recognized another of his kind. It came down to a sharing of small details: knowing how to string a racket, terms of address, dance steps, and so on.

The early settlers could not avoid the predatory outside world completely. As their numbers grew, their presence was accepted as inevitable and their status became legal. But they found that their rights to the inshore fishing, their only source of income, were used for bargaining in the diplomatic haggles between England and France. Starting from Utrecht in 1713, a series of treaties and accords were sternly implemented by the navies of both powers, and the fishermen in turn lost and regained their fishing grounds. It was not until an Anglo-French convention in 1904 that France, in exchange for territorial concessions in central Africa and a payment of money, gave up her fishing rights in Newfoundland.

The other main problems were partly internal, stemming from the very earliest days: the financial slavery of the fishermen to the planters, and the convergent evolution of a feudal system in the New World.

Two World Wars left the northern outports relatively unscathed; although the more accessible communities did provide brave cannon fodder, volunteers who mustered in the same spirit as led them to go on the great seal hunts. Yet seal hunting was practically as hazardous as going to war and certainly played a greater part in the development of outport life. The hunt was an annual carnage on the ice of the Labrador Current, and at the beginning of the twentieth century it had almost gained pilgrimage status. Men walked from as far as the Great Northern Peninsula of Newfoundland in order to compete for places on the vessels that went every year to the ice, where for a month or more they wrought bloody havoc on the seal herds and lived in unbelievably spartan conditions and filth. The ritual came to be more important than any financial incentive the men had for going "swiling," and even today seals are killed in unprofitable and dangerous ventures that are like compulsive sport.

The seal hunts caused migration and the imports of new ideas into the traditional communities. Their influence on the development of the outports was shared by the exploitation of the forests and, of course, fishing.

Logging operations began early in the 1900s, firstly by family units, each man and his sons cutting his own patch, then as commercially run camps. These had to be near water as the transportation of wood was by sea, and they were usually deep in the bays, far from the fishing. It is my impression that the people of the lumber settlements were of a different type to those who had remained true to the sea. They seemed to have more Indian blood, with darker complexions and less sociable ways, as though they had genetic reasons for shunning the salt water.

Briefly, then, this is how the outports came about, and it helps to explain their isolation and, to an outsider, their air of fantasy in the survival of a culture long since vanished in the West European countries that supplied the early settlers. But the outports were not as cut off as might at first be thought. Their people were capable seamen and had mobility as searchers of more profitable fishing grounds, and, farther afield, in the salt fish trade with the West Indies, and other deep-sea trading; they were certainly aware of the outside world. But they were indifferent to it rather than shy or fearful; strangers, as I have pointed out, received a hearty welcome despite the built-in elements of reserve. There were radios and occasionally television. I sat with one family and watched "American Man" take his first step on the moon and listened to the talk in the same room which was about the price of fish. For most of them the real world ended at the horizon and I found very little interest except in what was topical or meaningful in their daily lives.

Another, perhaps surprising, phenomenon in such a lively people was the absence of any consistent ethnic art. Possibly it is because of the perpetual impermanent nature of their settlements that their spirit has produced a distinctive flavour but no set dishes. There is no decorative art and, during my time there, commercial country and western music had supplanted the old modes of Celtic and English folk songs that were their musical traditions. Boat building was the nearest approach to art, for the boats were beautiful and the real pride in them reflects the creative experience of their construction.

The area produced only raw materials, there being no processing of any of the produce except in sparse instances of the fish plants, or packing stations, and there was thus no work other than fishing, lumbering, and seasonal labouring. Where there were roads there were jobs to be found with the Department of Highways, and the hospital, nursing stations, and schools accounted for others.

In one sense, therefore, the people of the coast were exploited to the full, the men working as unorganized labourers to catch fish and hew wood; they were, however, not only deprived of any share in the chain of affluence that resulted from their toil, from sealskin coats to fish sticks, but they were also at the mercy of the merchants who bought and shipped out their produce with all the advantages of a monopoly. But in another sense, the people of the coast were free from exploitation. They had only fish and wood to offer the world; the world took their offerings and left them alone. Because the process had gone on for three hundred years, a status quo had been reached, and although the people were materially poor, they were independent and had richness of spirit.

One reason for this lies in the abundant natural resources there were for the taking: birds and fish to eat, land for buildings and gardens, berries to be picked, moose and caribou to be hunted, wood for houses and burning. Nor, until very recently, had there been any bureaucracy to enmesh them and classify their plunder of the land. A rider to this situation was that there was no development of a middle class and no resultant fragmentation of aims and frittering away of outport unity.

Another reason could be found in the calibre of the men and women who gave rise to the Newfoundland stock: people with the initiative to survive in the new-found land that only surrendered its fruits to the hardiest. Then there was the very nature of the work itself, often pressing to the point of survival, rarely lacking in physical danger, that kept the original qualities honed, ensuring that the stock remained independent and resourceful.

The outports looked like poor, disorganized clusters of little frame houses in an often desolate, treeless setting. But the houses were warm and comfortable, and the poverty an illusion caused by the absence of ready cash and a natural distaste for display. Banks were few and far between, and most people relied on the merchant for credit for their fishing gear, and for food, hardware, and clothes. This often resulted in the fisherman handing over his fish at the end of the year and coming out of the deal without a spare dollar in his pocket. There was a scarcity of cash around; the dollar notes in circulation were tattered, thinned, and patched.

The metastases of a more materialistic, North American culture were showing themselves, as Detroit motor cars, electrical goods, household gadgetry, and fashionable clothes appeared, but the purchases were made more for novelty than status. For the outports, the criterion of success for a family was to be able to settle its bills at the store and be stocked with supplies enough to last the winter. A man could be employed for six months a year, collect dole throughout the winter, and still regard himself as successful. There was enough to do in order to organize the essentials of life – food, warmth, and shelter – to keep him busy and maintain his self-respect.

The source of this self-respect was the traditional way of

life, which was based on willingness to work and independence, themselves qualities gleaned from centuries of exploitation and privation. The last great theft, in an established line of thefts, may be the embezzlement of the spirit of this unknown corner of the world. In an effort to make it easier and cheaper to provide them with education and communications, the outport people were clumped together in resettlement programs, the smaller communities leaving their traditional coves and regrouping in designated areas as larger settlements. This brought a way of life to an end, but whether it will be the last confidence trick of all is another matter.

A GLOSSARY OF LOCAL WORDS
AND EXPRESSIONS

A

Abse: An abscess.

All beat out: Very tired.

B

Bakeapples: Cloudberries (Rubus chamaemorus L.) that grow on low shrubs on the hillsides. The plant is of the rose family. The berries look like an orange raspberry when ripe and have an earthy taste that some do not like. I found them delicious, fresh in pies or bottled.

Ballycatters: Ridges of ice formed by the tides that encrust the seashore.

Bedlamer: Second-year seal, thought to come from "bete de la mer." Also, a young boy, a youth, or early teen.

Bird: A penis, and, in small boys, the scrotum, too.

Blackberries: Crowberries (Empetrum nigrum L.) found on the hillside on low shrubs. They can be extremely plentiful, and are good fresh and in pies.

Boil-up: A meal or a cup of tea cooked outside, in a boat or in the woods. Also referred to as mug-up.

Born: To deliver a baby, as in "Who borned your baby, Dorcas?"

Breeze of wind: Can, and usually does, mean a gale.

Bring your music: Bring a musical instrument.

Buckle: To bend, spoken of a joint in a limb, as in, "I finds a rising in the knee and can't buckle it."

Buddy: Another person, even a stranger.

Bun: Biscuit.

Bun of bread: A loaf of bread.

C

Cannister: Often used for cancer.

Cantle: Quintal, a measure of fish, 112 lbs. by weight.

Captain: Sometimes the name given to the man who cooks on the boat.

Chest: Breasts (pronounced *brestes*).

Choked up on the stomach: A chest infection, like bronchitis, usually with a cough.

Civil weather: Pleasant weather.

Clever boat: A big or stoutly built boat.

Comed: Past tense of came.

Complaint: Diarrhea.

Corruption: Pus. A woman in Forteau, talking of a discharging wound, described it as having the "running evil."

Crackie: A little pet dog.

Cranky: Unsteady, said of a chair that once unseated me.

Crew: Family, or a group of closely related people.

Crooked: Fretful, often used to describe restless children.

Crowd: A family. "I got ten in my crowd."

Cruising down the shore: A visiting trip to other settlements along the coast.

Cuddy: A shelter in the bow of a boat.

Cup of tea: Can mean a large meal.

D

Daybed: A couch, often with a thin mattress, found in most Newfoundland kitchens.

Do a step: To dance.

Dodge: To walk from one place to another. "By 'n by, buddy dodged on over to Uncle George's house."

Dog: A team dog of the husky type.

Doned: Past tense of do. "We doned good for a while, sir."

Down the shore: Also "down north," along the coast toward the North.

Drug: A loop of chain for a komatik brake.

Duckish: The early part of the evening, the dusk.

E

Evening: Afternoon.

Eye dentist: Opthalmologist.

F

Falled: Past tense of fall. "A big stick of wood (tree trunk) falled on un."

Feel best kind: To feel well.

Feel smart: To "feel smart" is also to feel well, but to smart means to feel pain.

Find: To feel or suffer, as in "I finds my side," meaning "I have a pain in my side."

Flash: A flush or reddening.

Fleet of nets: A group of nets in one place.

Flipper pie: Pie filled with the meat of seal flippers, a traditional seasonal luxury.

Fly: A blackfly.

Foolish: Something that doesn't make sense, as in "We heard there's men on the moon. That's foolish, sure."

Foot wrists: Ankles (pronounced *wristes*).

Footing: The condition of the snow on the trails used for dog travel and skidooing.

Frosty: Cold or very cold.

G

Gansy: A woollen sweater, presumably derived from guernsey.

Garden: A place where only potatoes are grown.

Gas: A general term for indigestion.

Gathered: Infection, with redness and soreness, also called a rising.

Glitter: An ice storm, descriptive, as in the intense cold, ice crystallizes directly in the air.

Glutch: To swallow.

Growler: A free, mostly submerged lump of ice, up to the size of a small house, awash, and dangerous because it can be difficult to see.

Grumps: Bollards for attaching lines from a boat to the stages.

H

Handy on: Approximately or near.

Hauling nets: The act of pulling nets to take out the catch.

Heft: To assess the weight of an object by holding it.

Hove: Past tense of the verb heave, often used instead of throw. "He hove it in the water."

Husky: An Eskimo dog.

I

Ice: Any ice from a cube to a huge iceberg.

Ice-blink: The sign of ice over the horizon. The pack is reflected in the low distant sky as a pale yellow line.

J

Jigging hook or jigger: A lead fish about six inches long with two hooks curving from its mouth and a line attached to its tail. It is used without bait to catch codfish.

Job: Feces.

K

Killick: An anchor made by lashing staves of wood to form a cage and putting a small rock into it, used for anchoring nets.

Kitch: A stitch, or a shooting pain.

Knob: A lump.

Komatik: A sled.

L

Land bear: The black bear.

Let up: When a breeze dies down it "lets up."

Lop: Waves on water in a confined area, caused by wind.

Love child: An illegitimate child. In the ouports there was no stigma to be born out of wedlock.

Lunch: A meal or a snack at any time of the day or night.

M

Machine: A general-purpose noun that can be substituted for any sense. It is the Newfoundland equivalent of thingamajig.

Maid: A young girl.

Mesh: Low-lying marshy ground.

Mild weather: Foggy. It is also made into a noun. "A mild."

Monthlies: Menstrual periods.

N

Neck: A strip of land between two bodies of water.

Nerve doctor: A psychiatrist.

New ice: Ice that is just forming. It is often not consolidated and is unsafe.

Night: Evening.

Nip: To grip tightly or to crush. A boy "nips his sister's wrists" and hurts her.

Nipped: To be caught and trapped (in pack ice).

Nipper: A mosquito.

O

Old ice: Ice that formed at the beginning of winter. Toward the spring it becomes "rotten."

Once: Straightaway, as in "Come here the once."

P

Pans of ice: The constituents of the pack ice.

Partridgeberries: Sharp, red, currant-like berries (Vaccinium vitis-idaea L.) that are good in pies, called redberries in Labrador, and mountain cranberries, foxberries, or lingonberries elsewhere.

Penguins: Great Auks, now sadly extinct.

Pickle: Salted water.

Pinnacle tea: Tea made from water scooped from pans of Arctic pack ice, which consists of fresh water or from the pinnacles of icebergs.

Pitch back: To subside, used of swelling.

Plantation: A fishing settlement that would have been originally financed by a merchant or a planter.

Poll: The back of the head, usually specific to the occiput.

Pond: A lake.

Poor, or poorly: When used to describe a person or animal means thin.

Prong: Pitchfork used for handling fish.

Puff pig: A dolphin or "jumper."

Punishing: A pain can be described as "smarting" or "punishing," the latter used intransitively, depending on the severity of the pain or the stoicism of the sufferer.

Punts and skiffs: Small open boats propelled by oars or small motors.

R

Rackets: Snowshoes.

Rafted: Lifted up, used to describe pans of ice that are stacked up on each other because the pack is under pressure, as when it is blown onshore.

Rampse: A verb used of the boisterous playing of children, from "romping."

Regarding: Often used in the sense of concerning. "Regarding of that, I ain't feared of spooks."

Rising: A swelling.

Run: Body of water formed like a tickle, but much longer and wider.

S

Salt salmon: Can mean to ice down salmon or seal pelts.

Salve: Ointment or any medicine applied externally.

Saucy: Spiteful, mostly spoken of dogs.

Scattered: Occasional. A man out hunting for seals might say, "I seed the scattered one," if seals were scarce.

Scoop: A bailer for a boat.

Sea hounds: Porpoises.

Second hand: A nursing assistant.

Seed: Saw. "I seed your mother yesterday."

Sended: Used for sent. "We sended away fer it."

Shareman: A man who goes to fish with other men, often in a distant community, and takes a share in the proceeds of the catch.

Short-winded: Breathlessness.

"Sit down, b'ys": "Come and sit at the table, boys."

Skipper: The senior man on a boat, also used as a term of respect, on or off the water.

Slob: Slushy snow, or for thickening seawater as ice begins to form on it.

Slob hauler: An outmoded means of propulsion of a small boat in slob.

Smarting: A pain can be described as "smarting" or "punishing," the latter used intransitively, depending on the severity of the pain or the stoicism of the sufferer.

Some: Used as an adjective in place of "very," as in "some wonderful pain" or of food being "some good."

Sort out: To untangle dog traces or lines.

Spell: Time taken off, to take a rest, usually involving doing a small job for a change from a big one. The inference is that the fishermen never have any true time off.

Splits: Pieces of chopped firewood, shaved to make easier to start a fire with them. The shaving is called feathering.

Spruce partridge: A grouse.

Square flipper: A larger breed of seal, its skin used for the soles of boots.

Starved: To suffer. Starved with the cold means the person is freezing with the cold.

Stomach: A vague anatomical term describing the body from the neck to the pelvis. Thus, "I finds me stomach" could lead to a diagnosis anywhere from a heart attack to appendicitis.

Sunker: A submerged reef or rocks.

T

Tap on the head: A blow hard enough to knock one out.

Thousands: Plentiful. "Thousands of ice" means the ice is very thick in that place.

Tickle: A stretch of water between an island and the mainland or between two islands.

Tight to: Refers to something close, as in "tight to the northerner shore," meaning close to the north shore.

Trap boat: A larger, open boat, up to thirty feet long and eight or nine feet in the beam, propelled by an inboard engine, an all-purpose fishing boat, mainly used for hauling cod traps.

Trim: To whip, or a stick on a sled dog.

Turr: The Atlantic common murre, found all along the coast, and often served up. It tastes like a slightly fishy duck.

Twelvemonth: A year later. June twelvemonth means a year after June.

Twillick: A fairly common wader of the seashore, the Greater Yellow Legs.

U

Uncle: A term of respect used for an older man. He did not have to be a biological uncle.

Up: South.

V

Vexed: Could mean sorry as well as angry. "She was vexed with the maid" meant she was angry with her daughter, but if she was "Vexed for the maid," she was sorry for her.

W

Water bear: Polar bear.

Water pups: Boils that appear on the wrists of a saltwater fisherman.

While: Soon, as in, "I'll be there the while."

Wonderful: Often used as a superlative adjective, as in "wonderful good" and also a "wonderful pain."

Wrinkles: Periwinkles.

Y

Yumonie: Pneumonia.

INDEX

Miles Frankel was born in Romford, Essex, England, the first child of Eric and Constance Frankel. He spent most of his formative years growing up in Wanstead, London. He studied medicine at the London Hospital Medical College, graduated in 1967, and worked as a houseman in Poplar Hospital in London's Docklands. Following this he joined the Grenfell Mission in Newfoundland and Labrador. This appointment lasted two years and required much travelling by car, plane, skidoo, dog team, and on foot to provide care to isolated populations over a huge geographical area. He married Frances Astor in St. Anthony in 1970. From Canada they went to Paris for a year, where Miles worked in the American hospital, and they lived aboard their boat, *Conche*, on the Seine. During this time his brother Stephen had been working and researching in the highlands of Papua New Guinea and required a locum to concentrate further on his research, which Miles filled for ten months following his time in Paris.

In 1973, he took up a general practice post in rural North County Cork, Ireland, and lived and worked there for almost forty years until his retirement in 2011. Apart from medicine, he spent much of his time farming. He was introduced to horses by his current partner, Emer Ramsden, and took a keen interest in hunting. This interest evolved into working with horses, specifically the Percheron breed, and from the mid-1990s they established a stud. In the years following retirement, Miles and Emer spent much of their time in Ceret, in the western French Pyrenees.

Miles Frankel died in November 2014. He is survived by Emer and Frances, sons Gavin, Conrad, Conor, and Patrick, his brother Stephen, his grandchildren, Suji, Jacob, Corali, Constance, Thomas, and Ruairi, and extended family, Killian, Clare, and Roland.